DATE DUE

German in Review

German in Review

A Concise Survey of Grammar

FOURTH EDITION WITH EXERCISE MANUAL

Robert O. Röseler

UNIVERSITY OF WISCONSIN

HOLT, RINEHART AND WINSTON
NEW YORK   TORONTO   LONDON

Preface

From the Third Edition of *German in Review:*

Whether the objective in a language course be the ability to converse in the foreign language or the ability to read with ease, comprehension and enjoyment, experience has shown that the teaching of grammatical forms cannot be neglected without simultaneously neglecting a very vital part of the student's training. Therefore, it is my conviction that grammar has a definite place in the teaching of a foreign language just as do the teaching of pronunciation, the acquisition of a vocabulary, the development of fluency in reading, skill in writing, and oral proficiency.

Grammar shows the student the regularity in a mass of forms which otherwise would appear to be an unfathomable chaos of confusing irregularities. A too hasty and cursory treatment of grammar in the earlier stages of teaching a modern foreign language is certain to result later in lack of comprehension; the student is likely to find himself in distress whenever a reading selection demands of him an exact analysis of an involved sentence. So long as grammatical forms are necessary for exact understanding, especially in as richly inflected a language as German, essential forms of grammar need to be taught and need as frequent a systematic review as do vocabulary and the use of idioms.

Regardless of how much we advocate learning grammar inductively in a beginner's course, we know just as surely that in the second, third, or fourth semester of study the student must have and will ask for a systematic knowledge of grammar, since he cannot remember the multitudinous facts except in groupings, governed by principles. We recognize fully that these principles must be securely grasped and retained by the student but only on the basis of acquired linguistic habits and not on that of pure memory work: not grammar for its own sake, but grammar as a means to an end, with the stress placed upon functional rather than upon theoretical grammar.

The Fourth Edition of *German in Review:*

German in Review, Fourth Edition, is intended for German classes which have completed their basic study in German and have started to read German texts. It furnishes a systematic review of grammatical principles of the German language with diversified exercises in pattern drill, substitution drills, and German to English and English to German exercises, suitable for intermediate courses in German. The book may be used either as a supplement in reading courses, where a part of the teaching period is set aside for a short review of a chapter of grammar, or in grammar and composition courses.

Features of this edition:

1. The arrangement of the subject matter is topical so that the important facts about each grammatical principle may be found in one place. Most

sections occupy one or two pages, constituting a day's lesson for the average class, and containing but a single topic to keep the attention of the student for that day upon one point of grammar.

2. Although the sections are grouped under topical headings, they can be assigned in the order which will best meet the immediate needs of the class, since each section is a complete unit.

3. The various sections begin with illustrative paradigms or sentences from which the concise grammatical rules which follow are derived.

4. The comprehensive *Table of Contents* and complete *Index* facilitate rapid reference to any topic to which the student's attention has been directed.

Based on suggestions and recommendations of many instructors who have used *German in Review*, Third Edition, the following changes have been made in this new Fourth Edition:

1. Since an Exercise Manual supplements this edition, the number of exercises in each section has been reduced. The whole grammar review can easily be completed in one semester.

2. A tape program, with exercises adapted from the Exercise Manual, accompanies the text.

3. To make this new Fourth Edition strictly a "Grammar Review", dealing with nothing but the grammatical principles of the German language, the illustrative reading selections, the less important sections on phrase-compounds, derivations of verbs and nouns by a suffix or a prefix, and the sections on word study have not been included in this edition.

It is the desire and great pleasure of the author to express his most cordial thanks to the many friends and colleagues who have used the first editions of *German in Review* and who have so generously assisted by pertinent corrections and suggestions in the revision and completion of this new Fourth Edition of *German in Review*.

Madison, Wisconsin   R. O. R.

Table of Contents

THE CONJUNCTION

WORD ORDER

SYNOPSIS OF GRAMMAR

VOCABULARIES

INDEX

THE VERB

1 · Present Tense—Personal Endings
Indicative—Active

FIRST PERSON	SECOND PERSON	THIRD PERSON
ich frage	du fragst Sie fragen	er, sie, es fragt
wir fragen	ihr fragt Sie fragen	sie fragen
ich antworte	du antwortest Sie antworten	er, sie, es antwortet
wir antworten	ihr antwortet Sie antworten	sie antworten

a. The present tense, indicative active, of a German verb is formed by adding the following endings to the stem of the verb:

-e;   -st,   -en;   -t
-en;   -t,   -en;   -en

b. As an aid in pronunciation the connecting vowel -e- is added in the second and third person singular and the second person plural to verbs whose stem end in -t, -d, -n preceded by a consonant: **warten - wartest, finden - findest, bitten - bittest, antworten - antwortest.** (exception is the verb **lernen**: ich lerne, du lernst, er lernt).

A. *Supply the proper form of the verb in parentheses in each of the following sentences:*

1. Der Lehrer (fragen), und ich (antworten).
2. Ich (gehen) um halb neun zur Schule.
3. Wann (gehen) du zur Schule?
4. Warum (kommen) du immer zu spät zur Schule?
5. Wie (gehen) es deinem Vater?
6. Danke, es (gehen) ihm gut.
7. (Verstehen) ihr kein Deutsch, warum (antworten) ihr mir nicht?
8. Wir (schreiben) und (bitten) um schnelle Antwort.
9. Du (kommen) und (warten) auf mich.
10. Ich (sehen), du (glauben) mir nicht.
11. Du (sagen) nicht die Wahrheit, du (schaden) dir nur.
12. Ich (reisen) nicht, ich (bleiben) zu Hause.

2 · Past Tense of Weak Verbs*
Indicative—Active

FIRST PERSON	SECOND PERSON	THIRD PERSON
ich fragte	du fragtest Sie fragten	er, sie, es fragte
wir fragten	ihr fragtet Sie fragten	sie fragten
ich antwortete	du antwortetest Sie antworteten	er, sie, es antwortete
wir antworteten	ihr antwortetet Sie antworteten	sie antworteten

Weak verbs form the past tense by adding the suffix -te to the stem of the verb. If the stem ends in -t, -d, -m, -n, preceded by a consonant, the suffix -ete is added.**

A. *Rewrite the following sentences, using past tense:*
1. Wir lernen heute ein neues Gedicht auswendig.
2. Ich frage nach dem Namen des Dichters.
3. Er antwortet mir nicht auf meine Frage.
4. Warum antwortest du mir nicht auf meine Frage?
5. Erwartest du eine Antwort?
6. Wo ist Karl? Warum wartet er nicht auf mich?
7. Warten Sie auf mich?
8. Er sagt die Wahrheit, glauben Sie ihm nicht?
9. Sie reist nach Deutschland, ich wünsche ihr eine glückliche Reise.
10. Er redet viel, aber wir glauben ihm nicht.
11. Ich versuche zu arbeiten, aber der Lärm auf der Straße stört mich.
12. Er öffnet seine Bücher, aber er arbeitet nicht.

---

* The term *weak* and *strong* is intended to contrast those verbs which form their past tense by means of an internal vowel-change, called *ablaut*, thus seeming to rely upon their own strength, with those which have the "weakness" to rely upon foreign aid in the form of a suffix.
** For complete conjugation of a weak verb see *Synopsis of Grammar*, p.144.

3 · Past Tense of Strong Verbs
Indicative—Active

INFINITIVE	FIRST PERSON	SECOND PERSON	THIRD PERSON
singen	ich sang	du sangst Sie sangen	er, sie, es sang
	wir sangen	ihr sangt Sie sangen	sie sangen
schreiben	ich schrieb	du schriebst Sie schrieben	er, sie, es schrieb
	wir schrieben	ihr schriebt Sie schrieben	sie schrieben

Strong Verbs form the past tense by a change of the stem vowel. The first and third person singular drop the personal ending.*

A. *Supply the proper past tense forms of the verb:*

1. Ich ging gleich nach Hause.
2. Wir ____ gleich nach Hause.
3. Er ____ gleich nach Hause.
4. Ihr ____ gleich nach Hause.
5. ____ du gleich nach Hause?
6. ____ Sie gleich nach Hause?
7. ____ sie gleich nach Hause?
8. Ich fand das Buch.
9. Er ____ das Buch.
10. Wir ____ das Buch.
11. Wo ____ du das Buch?
12. Wo ____ ihr das Buch?
13. Wo ____ Sie das Buch?
14. Wann ____ er das Buch?

B. *Restate the following sentences in English:*

1. Die Kinder sangen ein altes deutsches Volkslied.
2. Wir blieben zwei Wochen bei den Großeltern.
3. Wir fuhren mit dem Auto nach New York.
4. Ich gab ihm all mein Geld.
5. Karl aß sein Frühstück und ging dann zur Universität.

---

* For vowel changes consult the list of strong verbs, p. 132.

THE VERB

C. *Restate the following sentences in German:*

1. We stayed with the grandparents all day (*den ganzen Tag*).
2. I met her at the theater, and we drove home together (*nach Hause*).
3. They spoke and read German very well (*sehr gut*).
4. He stood at (*am*) the window, held a book in his hand and read.
5. I came home late, sat a while by the stove, wrote a letter, and went to bed.

4 · Past Participle of Weak Verbs

INFINITIVE	PAST PARTICIPLE	INFINITIVE	PAST PARTICIPLE
fragen	gefragt	sagen	gesagt
arbeiten	gearbeitet	öffnen	geöffnet
studieren	studiert	regieren	regiert

a. Weak verbs form the past participle by adding the prefix **ge-*** and the suffix **-t** to the stem of the verb.**

A. *Give the past participle of the following weak verbs:*

1. bauen glauben stellen lernen fragen hören
2. klagen wählen leben lachen reisen zählen

B. *Supply the past participle of the verbs in parentheses:*

1. Wir haben vor einem Jahr dieses Haus (bauen).
2. Ich habe meine Aufgabe für morgen (lernen).
3. Meine Eltern haben lange in dieser Stadt (leben).
4. Er hat die Schultage bis zu den Ferien (zählen).
5. Wir haben einen neuen Präsidenten (wählen).

b. If the stem of the verb ends in **-t, -d, -n,** the suffix **-et** is added.

C. *Give the past participle of the following verbs:*

1. heiraten warten rechnen fürchten läuten retten
2. beten atmen bilden dichten ernten mieten

D. *Supply the past participle of the verbs in parentheses:*

1. Fräulein Müller hat gestern Herrn Mayer (heiraten).
2. Ich habe gestern auf dich (warten).
3. Er hat viele schöne Balladen (dichten).
4. Sie haben gestern in der Kirche um Regen (beten).
5. Unser Nachbar hat in diesem Herbst viel Korn (ernten).

---

* *See* rule **c.**
** For complete conjugation of a weak verb see *Synopsis of Grammar*, p. 144.

c. Verbs ending in **-ieren** drop the prefix **ge-** but retain the suffix **-t.**

E. *Give the past participle of the following verbs:*

1. zensieren   korrigieren   regieren   fabrizieren
2. kultivieren   exportieren   dirigieren   telephonieren

F. *Supply the past participle of the verbs in parentheses:*

1. Diese Fabrik hat kleine Motoren (fabrizieren).
2. Königin Victoria hat über sechzig Jahre lang (regieren).
3. Unser Professor hat unsere Arbeiten noch nicht (korrigieren).
4. Vater hat gestern von New York (telephonieren).
5. Unser Land hat in diesem Jahre mehr (exportieren) als (importieren).

5 · Past Participle of Strong Verbs

INFINITIVE	PAST PARTICIPLE	INFINITIVE	PAST PARTICIPLE
fallen	gefallen	sehen	gesehen
binden	gebunden	helfen	geholfen
sitzen	gesessen	treffen	getroffen

Strong verbs form the past participle by adding the prefix **ge-** and the suffix **-en** to the stem of the verb. Most strong verbs change the stem-vowel in forming the past participle.*

A. *Give the past participle of the following verbs:*

1. bleiben   schreiben   reiten   ziehen   fliegen   schwimmen
2. schließen   sterben   singen   lesen   fahren   fallen

B. *In the following sentences supply the past participle of the verbs in parentheses:*

1. Er ist heute lange in der Schule (bleiben).
2. Sie sind vor einem Jahr nach Californien (ziehen).
3. Sie hat heute abend besser als sonst (singen).
4. Wir sind nach der Vorlesung sofort nach Hause (gehen).
5. Ich bin über den Fluß ans andere Ufer (schwimmen).
6. Das Kind hat am See (spielen) und ist ins Wasser (fallen).
7. Du hast dein Wort nicht (halten) und hast mir mein Geld nicht (bringen).
8. Ich habe das Buch aus der Bibliothek (leihen), ich habe es aber noch nicht (lesen).
9. Ich habe Marie heute in der Bibliothek (sehen), ich habe aber nicht mit ihr (sprechen).
10. Unser Nachbar ist lange krank (sein), er ist gestern (sterben).
11. Der Soldat ist in die Hände der Feinde (fallen).
12. Die Soldaten haben bunte Uniformen (tragen).

---

* For vowel changes consult the list of strong verbs, p. 132.
  For complete conjugation of a strong verb see *Synopsis of Grammar*, p. 146.

C. *Say it in German, using the present perfect tense:*

1. My students read this German play (*use:* Schauspiel).
2. She wore a beautiful dress.
3. He spoke softly and slowly in his lectures (*use:* Vorlesungen).
4. You were not in school today, where have you been?
5. Did you see the man? Yes, I saw him.
6. When did he die? He died yesterday afternoon.

6 · Changes in the Present Tense of Strong Verbs

INFINITIVE	FIRST PERSON	SECOND PERSON	THIRD PERSON
fahren	ich fahre	du fährst	er fährt
laufen	ich laufe	du läufst	er läuft

a. Strong verbs with the stem-vowel **-a-**, **-au-** change **-a-** to **-ä-** and **-au-** to **-äu-** in the second and third person singular.

A. *Conjugate the following strong verbs in the present tense singular:*

1. schlafen   fallen   wachsen   waschen   halten
2. fangen   raten   schlagen   tragen   braten

B. *Restate the following sentences, using 1) second person singular (**du**-form), 2) third person singular:*

1. Ich fahre mit dem Autobus zur Stadt.
2. Ich laufe schnell und hole ein Auto.
3. Ich trage diese Bücher zur Bibliothek zurück.

INFINITIVE	FIRST PERSON	SECOND PERSON	THIRD PERSON
helfen	ich helfe	du hilfst	er hilft
sehen	ich sehe	du siehst	er sieht

b. Most strong verbs with the stem-vowel **-e-** change **-e-** to **-i-** or **-ie-** in the second and third person singular.

C. *Conjugate the following strong verbs in the present tense singular:*

1. sprechen   treffen   nehmen   lesen   geben
2. sterben   brechen   werfen   stehlen   sehen

D. *Restate the following sentences, using 1) second person singular (**du**-form), 2) third person singular:*

1. Ich spreche morgen mit unserm Professor über diese Sache.
2. Ich esse heute in der Stadt zu Mittag.
3. Ich treffe Fräulein Müller nach der Vorlesung.

INFINITIVE	FIRST PERSON	SECOND PERSON	THIRD PERSON
essen	ich esse	du ißt	*but:* er ißt
schließen	ich schließe	du schließt	*but:* er schließt

c. Any verb, strong or weak, with the stem ending in a sibilant **-s, -es, -ß, -sch, -tz, -z** may contract in the second person singular of the present tense the sibilant of the stem with the **-s-** of the inflectional ending.

E. *Give the second person singular* (**du**-*form*) *of the following verbs:*

1. schießen, *to shoot*
2. tanzen, *to dance*
3. sitzen, *to sit*
4. heißen, *to be called*
5. reißen, *to tear*
6. gießen, *to pour*

7 · <u>Haben</u> as Auxiliary of Perfect Tenses

PRESENT PERFECT   PRESENT   PAST PERFECT

Ich kaufe das Kleid

ich **habe** das Kleid gekauft	ich **hatte** das Kleid gekauft
Sie **haben** das Kleid gekauft	Sie **hatten** das Kleid gekauft
du **hast** das Kleid gekauft	du **hattest** das Kleid gekauft
er **hat** das Kleid gekauft	er **hatte** das Kleid gekauft
wir **haben** das Kleid gekauft	wir **hatten** das Kleid gekauft
ihr **habt** das Kleid gekauft	ihr **hattet** das Kleid gekauft
sie **haben** das Kleid gekauft	sie **hatten** das Kleid gekauft

a. Haben is the auxiliary used in the forming of perfect tenses (the present perfect, the past perfect) of all transitive and most intransitive verbs.*

A. *Conjugate the following sentences in 1) the present perfect tense; 2) the past perfect tense:*

1. Ich suche das Klassenzimmer.
2. Ich verlor mein Geld.
3. Ich zähle die Tage.
4. Ich miete eine andere Wohnung.
5. Ich vergaß seinen Namen.
6. Ich folge seinem Rat.

B. *Restate the following sentences, using present perfect tense:*

1. Ich lese eine Novelle von Gottfried Keller.
2. Ich fühle mich unter den vielen Leuten nicht wohl.
3. Sie singt ein altes deutsches Volkslied.
4. Sie sah das schöne, teure Kleid und kaufte es.
5. Du teilst dein Geld und deine Zeit mit ihm.
6. Trägst du den Brief sofort zur Post?

C. *Restate in English:*

1. Er hat seine Abende und oft ganze Nächte seinen Studien in den Naturwissenschaften gewidmet (*devoted*), und er ist ein Mann von vielen Kenntnissen gewesen.
2. Die Menschen haben immer ein besseres Gedächtnis für das Unrecht gehabt, welches (*which*) sie haben leiden müssen, als (*than*) für das Unrecht, welches sie selber getan haben.

---

* For complete conjugation of the auxiliary **haben** see *Synopsis of Grammar*, p. 138.

          THE VERB

---

ich **werde** das Kleid gekauft **haben**
Sie **werden** das Kleid gekauft **haben**
du **wirst** das Kleid gekauft **haben**
Sie ~~er **wird**~~ das Kleid gekauft **haben**
wir **werden** das Kleid gekauft **haben**
ihr **werdet** das Kleid gekauft **haben**
sie **werden** das Kleid gekauft **haben**

---

b. Haben is also the auxiliary in the forming of the future perfect tense. The future perfect very often expresses presumption: **Er wird gestern den Brief geschrieben haben.** *He has probably written the letter yesterday.*

D. *Restate the following sentences, using future perfect tense:*

1. Er hat wahrscheinlich einen Kranken besucht.
2. Er bringt den Brief sofort zur Post.
3. Sie hat ihre Schularbeit nicht gemacht.
4. Er hat mich auf der Straße nicht erkannt.
5. Er hat die Einladung, uns zu besuchen, gewiß vergessen.

8 · <u>Sein</u> as Auxiliary of Perfect Tenses

Ich gehe zur Arbeit

ich **bin** zur Arbeit gegangen	ich **war** zur Arbeit gegangen
Sie **sind** zur Arbeit gegangen	Sie **waren** zur Arbeit gegangen
du **bist** zur Arbeit gegangen	du **warst** zur Arbeit gegangen
er **ist** zur Arbeit gegangen	er **war** zur Arbeit gegangen
wir **sind** zur Arbeit gegangen	wir **waren** zur Arbeit gegangen
ihr **seid** zur Arbeit gegangen	ihr **wart** zur Arbeit gegangen
sie **sind** zur Arbeit gegangen	sie **waren** zur Arbeit gegangen

a. Sein is the auxiliary used in forming the perfect tenses of <u>intransitive</u> verbs which denote a change in position: **begegnen, fahren, fallen, folgen, gehen, laufen, kommen, reisen, reiten, steigen, wandern.** *

A. *Conjugate the following sentences in 1) the present perfect tense; 2) the past perfect tense:*

1. Ich komme früh nach Hause.
2. Ich schwimme über den See.
3. Ich gehe zur Schule.
4. Ich reise nach Europa.
5. Ich fahre zur Stadt.
6. Ich ziehe nach Kalifornien.

B. *In the following sentences fill in the present perfect form of* **sein:**

1. Das Kind ____ vom Spielen müde geworden.
2. Wann ____ Ihr Zug in Chicago angekommen?
3. Warum ____ Sie nicht länger in New York geblieben?
4. Wo ____ du gestern abend gewesen?
5. Wann ____ Sie in Chicago angekommen?
6. Wann ____ er nach Mexiko abgereist?
7. ____ du allein über den Fluß geschwommen?
8. ____ ihr noch lange in der Stadt geblieben?
9. ____ heute keiner von euch zur Vorlesung gegangen?
10. ____ Sie auf Ihrer Reise auch in die Schweiz gekommen?

C. *Restate the following sentences, using present perfect tense:*

1. Er geht nie in ein Theater.
2. Er reitet noch heute abend nach Hause.
3. Viele Flugzeuge flogen heute über unsere Stadt.
4. Die Kinder liefen aus der Schule schnell nach Hause.

---

* For complete conjugation of the auxiliary **sein** see *Synopsis of Grammar*, p. 140.

5. Er sprang über den Graben und fiel ins Wasser.
6. Wir gingen zur Schule, und der Hund folgte uns.

Werden	Sein
ich **werde** hier krank	ich **bin** in der Schule
ich **wurde** hier krank	ich **war** in der Schule
ich **bin** hier krank **geworden**	ich **bin** in der Schule **gewesen**
ich **werde** hier krank **werden**	ich **werde** in der Schule **sein**
wir **werden** hier krank	wir **sind** in der Schule

b. **Sein** is also the auxiliary used in the forming of the perfect tenses of three verbs, denoting a change in condition: **werden** (*to become*), **wachsen** (*to grow*), **sterben** (*to die*) and in forming the perfect tenses of two verbs of rest: **sein** (*to be*), **bleiben** (*to stay*).

D. *Restate the following sentences, using 1) present perfect tense; 2) future tense:*

1. Es wird hier im Norden kalt.
2. Er wird in seinem Geschäft reich.
3. Sie wird jetzt mit ihrem Gelde sparsamer.
4. Rosen und Blumen wachsen nicht in unserm Garten.
5. Großvater starb an dieser Krankheit.
6. Wir bleiben den Winter über in Florida.
7. Ich bin jeden Abend zu Hause.
8. Wir sind in diesem Semester sehr fleißig.

> er **wird** spät nach Hause gekommen **sein***
> Sie **werden** spät nach Hause gekommen **sein**
> du **wirst** spät nach Hause gekommen **sein**
> er **wird** spät nach Hause gekommen **sein**
> wir **werden** spät nach Hause gekommen **sein**

c. **Sein** is also the auxiliary used in the forming of the future perfect tense of intransitive verbs. (See page 149)

E. *Restate the following sentences, using future perfect tense:*

1. Er ging wahrscheinlich in die Bibliothek.
2. Wir werden verreist sein.
3. Sie wird nach Hause gehen.
4. Unser Professor ist plötzlich krank geworden.

---

* *he probably came home late*

9 · The Use of the Present Perfect Tense

Friedrich der Zweite hat von 1740 bis 1786 in Preußen regiert.
Frederick the Second ruled in Prussia from 1740 to 1786.

George Washington ist der erste Präsident der Vereinigten Staaten gewesen.
George Washington was the first president of the United States.

The present perfect tense is regularly used in German to refer to a single event or situation in past time, where English would normally use the simple past tense.

A. *Say it in English:*

1. Vater ist gestern abend nicht zu Hause gewesen.
2. Mein Freund Karl hat im letzten Sommer viel Geld verdient.
3. Ich bin heute von der Universität zu Fuß nach Hause gegangen.
4. Wir sind nur ein paar Tage in Frankfurt geblieben.
5. Mein Vater und auch meine Mutter haben in Deutschland studiert.
6. Am 22. Juli 1831 hat Goethe sein großes Werk, den Faust, beendet.

B. *Restate in English:*

1. Er hat immer nur an seine eigenen Interessen gedacht, und hat nie ein Herz für die Leiden seiner Mitmenschen gehabt.
2. Der Kinder Hoffnung und Ideal ist immer der Jüngling, des Jünglings Hoffnung und Ideal ist immer der erfolgreiche Mann gewesen.
3. Immer nur wenige Menschen sind ganz frei von den Irrtümern ihres Jahrhunderts gewesen, auch sind sie in ihrem Haß ebenso verschieden gewesen wie (*as*) in ihrer Liebe.
4. „Die deutsche Musik hat viele herrliche, unvergleichliche Werke aufzuweisen, aber die italienische Musik ist auch so unendlich reich, so genial und eigentümlich, so ganz der Abglanz des ewig blauen Himmels Italiens."

   (A.F.J. Thibaut)
5. „Die Herren der Welt sind immer diejenigen gewesen, die im Kriege die Tapfersten und Stärksten, im Frieden aber die Weisesten und gerechtesten um sich versammeln konnten."

   (Goethe)

10 · Werden as Auxiliary of Future Tenses

FIRST PERSON	SECOND PERSON	THIRD PERSON
ich **werde** fragen	du **wirst** fragen	er **wird** fragen
wir **werden** fragen	ihr **werdet** fragen	sie **werden** fragen
ich **werde** bleiben	du **wirst** bleiben	er **wird** bleiben
wir **werden** bleiben	ihr **werdet** bleiben	sie **werden** bleiben

The present tense of **werden,** with the infinitive of the verb, is used in forming the future tense.*

A. *Supply the proper form of* **werden:**

1. Ich ____ heute abend zu Hause sein.
2. Er ____ uns um Hilfe bitten.
3. Wir ____ in der Stadt bleiben und dort essen.
4. Er ____ viel versprechen und wenig halten.
5. Ich fürchte, diese Arbeit ____ mir nicht gelingen.
6. Ihr ____ in der Galerie die schönsten Bilder sehen.
7. Ich fürchte, der Hund ____ mich beißen.
8. Das neue Semester ____ in zwei Wochen beginnen.
9. Warte auf mich, ich ____ gleich wieder zurück sein.
10. Ich weiß, sie ____ kommen, aber wann ____ sie kommen?
11. Ich ____ dir das Buch leihen, aber ich ____ es dir nicht schenken.
12. Wann denkst du, daß du mit dieser Studie fertig sein ____?

B. *Restate the following sentences, using the future tense:*

1. Ich nehme Ihre freundliche Einladung gerne an.
2. Ich folge diesem Befehl sehr ungern.
3. Wir verlassen diese Stadt höchst ungern.
4. Sie schickte deinen Ring und deine Briefe zurück.
5. Er kommt und entschuldigt sich.
6. Viele Leute kauften Karten zu dieser Vorstellung.
7. Wir schicken Ihnen sofort die gewünschte Summe.
8. Ihr sprecht mit eurem Vater über diesen Vorschlag.
9. Ihm fehlt das nötige Handwerkszeug zu dieser Arbeit.
10. Am 15. Juni beginnen meine Ferien, ich bleibe aber nicht zu Hause, ich suche mir Arbeit.

---

* For complete conjugation of the auxiliary **werden** see *Synopsis of Grammar*, p. 142.

11 · Verbs Compounded with an Inseparable Prefix

PRESENT	PAST	PRES. PERF.	3RD PERS. PRES.
bemerken	bemerkte	hat bemerkt	er bemerkt
entkommen	entkam	ist entkommen	er entkommt
erforschen	erforschte	hat erforscht	er erforscht
gehören	gehörte	hat gehört	er gehört
vergeben	vergab	hat vergeben	er vergibt
zerstören	zerstörte	hat zerstört	er zerstört

Verbs compounded with an inseparable prefix (**be-, ent-, er-, ge-, ver-, zer-**) form the past participle without the prefix **ge-**.

A. *Give the principal parts of the following verbs with inseparable prefix:*＊

1. bedenken   beantworten   begegnen   bedienen
2. entlassen   entscheiden   entdecken   entgegnen
3. erziehen   erzählen   erkranken   erhalten
4. gefallen   gelingen   gewöhnen   gebieten
5. verkaufen   verreisen   verdienen   verstehen
6. zerstören   zerschneiden   zerreißen   zerbrechen

B. *Supply the past participle in the following answers:*

1. Erzählte er von seinen Reisen in Asien?
   Ja, er hat von seinen Reisen in Asien ＿＿＿.
2. Begleitetest du Marie nach Hause?
   Ja, ich habe Marie nach Hause ＿＿＿.
3. Gelang euch diese schwere Arbeit?
   Nein, diese schwere Arbeit ist uns nicht ＿＿＿.
4. Befreitet ihr diese Gefangenen?
   Ja, wir haben diese Gefangenen ＿＿＿.
5. Verkauften Sie Ihre Bücher?
   Nein, ich habe meine Bücher nicht ＿＿＿.
6. Zerstörte der Feind die Stadt?
   Ja, der Feind hat die Stadt ＿＿＿.
7. Erwarteten Sie heute Besuch?
   Nein, ich habe heute keinen Besuch ＿＿＿.

＊ For vowel changes consult the list of strong verbs, p. 132.

THE VERB

12 · Verbs Compounded with a Separable Prefix

> Wir **kamen** gestern von unserer Europareise **zurück**.
> Wir **nehmen** unsere Studien wieder **auf**.
>
> Wir sind gestern von unserer Europareise **zurückgekommen**.
> Wir haben unsere Studien wieder **aufgenommen**.

a. In simple tenses (the present and the past) the separable prefix of the compound verb goes to the end of the clause.

b. In the compound tenses (the present perfect, the past perfect, the future, and the future perfect) the separable prefix precedes the verb at the end of the clause and prefix and verb are written as one word.

The most common separable prefixes are:

ab-	ein-	mit-	um-	vor-
an-	fort-	nach-	unter-	weg-
auf-	heraus-	nieder-	zu-	wieder-
aus-	herein-	entgegen-	zurück-	zusammen-

A. *Restate the following sentences, using 1) the past tense; 2) the present perfect tense; 3) the future tense:*

1. Er geht langsam die Straße hinab.
2. Er kommt von einem Spaziergang zurück.
3. Er ruht von seinem Spaziergang aus.
4. Wie kommt er in das Haus hinein?
5. Warum bringen Sie nicht ihren Freund mit?
6. Warum brechen Sie ihre Freundschaft mit ihm ab?

B. *Restate the following sentences in German, using present perfect tense:*

1. He is leaving (*abreisen*) today.
2. He looked (*aussehen*) tired and sick.
3. I stopped (*aufhören*) with my work and closed (*zumachen*) my books.
4. We get together (*zusammenkommen*) quite often and prepare (*vorbereiten*) our lessons.
5. When did he drive away (*wegfahren*), and when did he return (*zurückkommen*)?
6. Sit down (*sich hinsetzen*) and rest (*ausruhen*) a little.

13 · Irregular Weak Verbs

PRESENT	PAST	PAST PARTICIPLE	3RD PERS. PRES.
brennen	brannte	gebrannt	er brennt
kennen	kannte	gekannt	er kennt
denken	dachte	gedacht	er denkt
bringen	brachte	gebracht	er bringt

a. The so-called irregular weak verbs: **brennen, kennen, nennen, rennen, senden, wenden, denken, bringen** have vowel changes in the past tense and the past participle like strong verbs, and have endings like weak verbs. **Denken** and **bringen** also change the final consonants of the stem.*

A. *Restate the following sentences in 1) the past tense; 2) the present perfect tense:*

1. Die ganze Stadt brennt.
2. Ich kenne den Mann nicht.
3. Nennen Sie mir Ihren Namen?
4. Ich sende Ihnen die gewünschten Waren.
5. Ich denke noch oft an die schönen Zeiten.
6. Er denkt nicht mehr an sie.
7. Ich bringe Ihnen das gewünschte Geld.
8. Bringen Sie mir das gewünschte Buch?

Ich weiß, wer er ist.	wir wissen, wer er ist
du weißt, wer er ist.	ihr wißt, wer er ist.
er weiß, wer es ist.	sie wissen, wer es ist.

b. The present tense of **wissen** is irregular in the singular. Both **wissen** and **kennen** mean *to know;* **kennen** in the sense of *to be acquainted with*, **wissen** in the sense of *to have knowledge of a fact.*

---

* See *Synopsis of Grammar*, p. 136.

B. *Supply the proper form of* **wissen** *or* **kennen** *in the present tense:*

1. ____ du, wie spät es ist?
2. ____ du dieses Mädchen?
3. ____ du ihre Eltern?
4. ____ du, wo sie wohnt?
5. Nein, das ____ ich nicht.

6. ____ du, wer dieser Mann ist?
7. Nein, das ____ ich nicht.
8. ____ du diesen Professor?
9. Ja, ich ____ ihn.
10. Nein, ich ____ ihn nicht.

C. *Say it in German:*

1. Do you know this child?
2. Do you know the city?
3. I don't know his address.
4. I don't know her birthday.
5. I don't know her parents.
6. I don't know the story, I never read it.

7. I know the story, but I don't know the name of the author.
8. I know the street, but I don't know the number of the house.
9. I know where he lives, and I know the number of the house.

14 · Impersonal Verbs

es regnet — *it's raining*	wie spät ist es? — *what time is it?*
es gefällt mir — *I like it*	es läutet — *the doorbell is ringing*
es brennt — *there is a fire*	es freut mich — *I am glad*

a. In German, as in English, many verbs are used impersonally with the grammatical subject **es** (*it*).

A. *Study and memorize the following German phrases and sentences with the impersonal* **es:**

1. es scheint mir — *it seems to me*
   es gefällt mir nicht — *I don't like it*
   es tut mir leid — *I am sorry*
   es ärgert mich — *I am vexed*
   es geht mir gut — *I am fine*

2. es klingt nicht gut — *it doesn't sound right*
   es sieht nicht gut aus — *it doesn't look good*
   es ist schwer zu sagen — *it's hard to say*
   es fragt sich — *the question is whether*
   es klopft — *somebody is knocking*

3. es regnet draußen — *it's raining outside*
   es schneit — *it's snowing*
   es brennt in der Stadt — *there is a fire downtown*
   es friert mich — *I feel cold*
   es wird getanzt heute abend — *there is dancing tonight*

4. wie spät ist es? — *what time is it?*
   es ist halb acht — *it's half past seven*
   ist es spät? — *is it late?*
   es wird spät — *it's getting late*
   es ist schon zehn Uhr — *it's ten o'clock already*

5. Wir geht es Ihnen? — *How are you?*
   Wie geht es Ihrem Vater? — *How is your father?*
   Danke, es geht ihm gut. — *Thanks, he is well.*
   Wie gefällt es Ihnen hier? — *How do you like it here?*
   Es gefällt mir hier sehr gut. — *I like it here very much.*

B. *Say it in German:*

1. I am sorry, but I can't come.
2. Is it still raining?
3. No, it stopped. (*aufhören*)

4. Somebody is knocking at the door. (*klopfen*)
5. The bell is ringing. (*läuten*)
6. It doesn't look good. (*aussehen*)
7. Mother, what time is it?
8. It's twelve o'clock.
9. It's getting late.

---

ich bin es,   *it's I*   sie sind es,   *it's they*
er ist es,   *it's he*   er sagt es,   *he says so*

         wir sind es, die es getan haben
         it's we who did it

---

b. The pronoun **es** is also used as a completion of a predicate.

C. *Say it in English:*

1. Er meint es gut mit uns.
2. Ich habe es gut hier bei euch.
3. Ich bin es müde, weiter mit ihm zu unterhandeln.
4. Er ist ein tüchtiger Geschäftsmann, er hat es weit gebracht.
5. Hast du es getan? Nein, ich habe es nicht getan.

Es gibt viele sonnige Tage   — *There are many sunny days.*
Es gab heute keinen Regen — *There was no rain today.*
Es ist jemand an der Tür   — *There is somebody at the door.*
Es war einmal ein König   — *There was once upon a time a king.*

---

c. Es gibt and **es gab; es ist** and **es war** (*there is, there are; there was, there were*) express generalizations concerning conditions or facts which may be continuously or universally true.*

D. *Say it in English:*

1. Es gibt viele fleißige Leute in dieser Stadt. (*there are*)
2. Es gibt viele Sprachen in der Welt. (*there are*)
3. Es waren zwanzig sehr begabte Studenten in meiner Klasse. (*there were*)
4. Es gab mehr Männer als Frauen in diesem Lande. (*there were*)
5. Es gibt viele Sterne am Himmel. (*there are*)
6. Es sind fünf Schulen in dieser kleinen Stadt. (*there are*)

---

* **es ist** requires a nominative; **es gibt** requires an accusative object; **es geht, es scheint, es gefällt,** etc., require a dative object.

15 · Reflexive Verbs

	FIRST PERSON	SECOND PERSON	THIRD PERSON
Singular:	ich fürchte **mich**	du fürchtest **dich**	er fürchtet **sich**
Plural:	wir fürchten **uns**	ihr fürchtet **euch**	sie fürchten **sich**
Singular:	ich helfe **mir**	du hilfst **dir**	er hilft **sich**
Plural:	wir helfen **uns**	ihr helft **euch**	sie helfen **sich**

a. In reflexive constructions the personal pronouns are added to the verb. For the first and second person in the singular and plural the accusative or dative cases of the pronoun are used, for the third person of both the singular and the plural **sich** is used.*
The pronoun stands always directly after the inflective element.

A. *Supply the reflexive pronouns:*

1. ich setze ____; ich verstecke ____; ich wasche ____
2. du setzt ____; du versteckst ____; du wäscht ____
3. er setzt ____; er wäscht ____; er versteckt ____
4. wir setzen ____; ihr versteckt ____; sie waschen ____
5. Wir freuen ____ auf euren Besuch.
6. Ich irrte ____ in der Hausnummer.
7. Kümmert ____ um eure Gäste!
8. Er weigert ____, die Rechnung zu bezahlen.
9. Fürchtet ____ nicht vor den vielen Menschen.
10. Wir verlassen ____ auf eure Hilfe.

Das Buch gehört mir.	Ich glaube dir nicht.
Vertrauen Sie mir!	Glauben Sie mir!

b. Verbs taking the dative require a dative pronoun.

B. *Supply the reflexive pronouns in the dative case:*

1. Deine späte Hilfe nützt ____ nichts.
2. Er begegnete (*him*) auf der Straße.
3. Ich erlaube ____ zu fragen.
4. Ich nehme ____ vor zu reisen.

---

* For the complete conjugation of a reflexive verb see *Synopsis of Grammar*, p. 150.

5. Bilde _____ das nicht ein!
6. Suche _____ eine andere Arbeit!
7. Merke _____ seinen Namen!
8. Nimm _____ Zeit zu dieser Arbeit.

Verzeihen Sie! Ich habe mich geirrt.
Wir haben uns über ihn geärgert.
Ich habe mir eine Zigarette angezündet.

---

c. Since the pronoun is the object of the verb, reflexive verbs are regarded as transitive and use **haben** as their auxiliary.

C. *Restate in the present perfect tense:*

1. Ich sehne mich nach Ruhe.
2. Er weigert sich zu kommen.
3. Sie kümmert sich um ihre Gäste.
4. Die Kinder versteckten sich im Garten.
5. Wir gewöhnen uns an diese Hitze.
6. Ich kaufe mir einen neuen Hut.

D. *Restate the following sentences in German:*

1. I am pleased (*sich freuen*) to hear that you are well again.
2. Please take a chair and sit down (*sich setzen*).
3. I couldn't think of (*sich erinnern*) his name.
4. I got accustomed to (*sich gewöhnen*) the hot summers in the South.
5. Father had worked hard and was longing (*sich sehnen*) for a good rest.

16 · The Imperative

INFINITIVE	du-FORM	ihr-FORM	Sie-FORM
singen	singe! *or* sing!	singt!	singen Sie!
rufen	rufe! *or* ruf!	ruft!	rufen Sie!

   a. The imperative denotes a command. There is an imperative only for the second person singular and the second person plural.
The ending -e- of the **du**-form is often omitted: **sing! ruf! lauf!** The conventional address (**Sie**-form) always adds the pronoun **Sie: Singen Sie! Rufen Sie!**

A. *Give the three imperatives of the following phrases:*

1. Geduld haben   Mitleid haben   Ordnung haben
2. fleißig sein   ehrlich sein   pünktlich sein
3. sich freuen   sich weigern   sich nicht ärgern
4. Arbeit finden   Ruhe finden   Freunde finden
5. den Lehrer fragen   die Wahrheit sagen   den Arzt rufen

INFINITIVE	du-FORM	ihr-FORM	Sie-FORM
nehmen	nimm!	nehmt!	nehmen Sie!
sehen	sieh!	seht!	sehen Sie!

   b. Strong verbs which change the stem-vowel from -e- to -i- or to -ie- in the second and third person singular of the present tense have the same change in the second singular (the **du**-form) of the imperative and never add the ending -e.

B. *Give the three imperatives of the following phrases:*

1. das Geschenk nicht annehmen
2. sich das Schauspiel ansehen
3. dem Nachbar helfen
4. nicht so schnell essen
5. mich morgen treffen

    THE VERB

6. sich in acht nehmen
7. sich die Zeit nehmen
8. etwas lauter sprechen
9. etwas langsamer lesen
10. uns nicht vergessen

C. *Restate in German in the second person singular and plural:*

1. Stay here! (*hier bleiben*)
2. Go and see! (*gehen, sehen*)
3. Keep quiet! (*still sein*)
4. Forget it! (*vergessen*)
5. Stand still! (*still stehen*)
6. Sleep well! (*gut schlafen*)
7. Tell me! (*sagen mir*)
8. Ask him! (*fragen ihn*)
9. Come in! (*herein kommen*)
10. Hurry up! (*sich beeilen — euch*)

THE VERB

17 · Modal Auxiliaries

dürfen, *may, to be allowed to*	Darf ich jetzt gehen? *May I go now?*
können, *can, be able to*	Er kann nicht lesen. *He can't read.*
mögen, *like to, care to*	Ich mag ihn nicht. *I don't like him.*
müssen, *must, have to*	Ich muß ihm danken. *I have to thank him.*
sollen, *shall, to be expected to*	Was soll ich tun? *What shall I do?*
wollen, *will, shall, intend to*	Er will nicht kommen. *He doesn't want to come.*

a. Modal auxiliaries express the ideas of permission, possibility, obligation, compulsion, intention, etc.: *may, can, must, shall, should, could, care to.*

CONJUGATION OF MODALS:*

INFINITIVE	**dürfen**	**können**	**mögen**
PRESENT	ich **darf** *I may* du **darfst** er **darf** wir dürfen ihr dürft sie dürfen	**kann** *I can* **kannst** **kann** können könnt können	**mag** *I like to* **magst** **mag** mögen mögt mögen
PAST	ich durfte *I was allowed to*	konnte *I was able to*	mochte *I liked to*
PRESENT PERFECT	ich habe gedurft	gekonnt	gemocht
PAST PERFECT	ich hatte gedurft	gekonnt	gemocht
FUTURE	ich werde dürfen	können	mögen
FUTURE PERFECT	ich werde gedurft haben	gekonnt haben	gemocht haben

* For complete conjugation see *Synopsis of Grammar*, p. 152.

THE VERB

b. 1. Modal auxiliaries are irregular in the present tense singular.

2. The umlaut of **dürfen, können, mögen,** and **müssen** disappears in the past tense and in the past participle.

3. In all other tenses than the present the inflectional forms of the modal auxiliaries are identical with those of regular weak verbs.

A. *Conjugate in the present tense; follow the example:*

ich will nicht	ich soll nicht	ich mag nicht	ich darf nicht
du willst nicht	——	——	——
Sie wollen nicht	——	——	——
er will nicht	——	——	——
wir wollen nicht	——	——	——
ihr wollt nicht	——	——	——
sie wollen nicht	——	——	——

B. *Restate the following sentences in English:*

1. Darf (*use:* may) ich um ein Glas Wasser bitten?
2. Die Kinder dürfen (*use:* are allowed) im Garten aber nicht auf der Straße spielen.
3. Ich kann sehr gut Deutsch und Spanisch aber weder Französisch noch Russisch sprechen.
4. Das Kind starb, ehe der Vater einen Arzt holen konnte (*use:* was able).
5. Sie mag dieses Kleid nicht (*use:* doesn't like).
6. Sie mochten (*use:* didn't like to) über diese Sache nicht sprechen.
7. Alle seine Verwandten sollen (*use:* it is said) gestorben sein.
8. Sie sagt, daß sie um zehn Uhr zu Hause sein muß (*use:* has to be).
9. Du darfst (*use:* may) gehen, wenn du gehen willst (*use:* wish to).
10. Wollen Sie (*use:* would you) bitte Ihren Namen in dieses Buch eintragen.

C. *Restate the following sentences in past tense:*

1. Wir dürfen in seiner Wohnung nicht rauchen.
2. Sprechen Sie lauter, ich kann Sie nicht verstehen.
3. Ich mag sonntags nicht arbeiten.
4. Wir müssen uns sofort entscheiden, ob wir mitgehen wollen oder nicht.
5. Wie soll ich wissen, ob er die Wahrheit spricht.
6. Sie wollen von heute an um sechs Uhr aufstehen.
7. Ich will dir nur sagen, daß du sorgfältiger arbeiten sollst.
8. Die Kinder sagen, daß sie den neuen Lehrer nicht mögen.

THE VERB

Er hat das Haus gewollt.	*He wanted the house.*
Sie hat nach Hause gemußt.	*She had to go home.*
Ich habe es nicht gemocht.	*I didn't like it.*

c. The regular past participle with the prefix **ge-** is used when no dependent infinitive is expressed in the sentence.

Er hat das Haus kaufen wollen.	*He wanted to buy the house.*
Sie hat nach Hause gehen müssen.	*She had to go home.*
Ich habe es nicht lesen mögen.	*I didn't care to read it.*

d. When a dependent infinitive is expressed in the sentence, a past participle without **ge-** is used which is identical in form with the infinitive. This phrase, consisting of the dependent infinitive and the participle without **ge-** of the modal auxiliary, is commonly called the "double infinitive." It always stands last in a sentence.

D. *Restate in English:*

1. Ich habe diese Arbeit fertig machen müssen.
   Ich werde diese Arbeit fertig machen müssen.
2. Mein Vater hat mir helfen müssen.
   Mein Vater wird mir helfen müssen.
3. Er hat heute nicht arbeiten mögen.
4. Die alte Frau hat nicht schreiben können.
5. Wir haben gestern abend nicht ausgehen dürfen.
6. Ich habe zur Universität gehen wollen, als es zu regnen anfing.

E. *Restate the following sentences in German:*

1. Nobody is permitted to enter (*use:* dürfen).
2. He couldn't write his name (*use:* können).
3. He is said to be sick (*use:* sollen).
4. We are not allowed to stay longer (*use:* dürfen).
5. We must all die sometime (*use:* müssen).
6. I don't want to go home (*use:* wollen).
7. We didn't like the concert (*use:* mögen).
8. What are we to do now? (*use:* sollen).
9. I had to read this German story (*use:* müssen).

10. He is sick and I have not been able to see him (*use:* können).
11. Did you have to study last night? (*use:* müssen).
12. Didn't he want to help you? (*use:* wollen)

F. *Say it in English:*

1. „Es ist nicht genug zu wissen, man muß auch anwenden (*to apply*) können; es ist nicht genug zu wollen, man muß auch tun können."
   (Goethe)

2. „Wenn auch die Welt im ganzen fortschreitet (*progresses in general*), die Jugend muß doch immer wieder von vorne anfangen (*start anew from the beginning*) und als Individuum die Epochen der Weltkultur durchmachen."
   (Goethe)

3. „Wissenschaft (*science, learning*) ist wie ein großes Feuer, das in jedem Volke unaufhörlich (*incessantly*) unterhalten werden muß."
   (Freytag)

4. „Kein freier Mann soll ergriffen, oder soll gefangen gesetzt, oder soll seines Landes oder seiner Freiheit beraubt, geächtet, verbannt oder sonst wie vernichtet werden. Niemandem wollen oder dürfen wir Recht und Gerechtigkeit verkaufen, verweigern oder versagen."
   ("Magna Charta")

18 · Double Infinitive Constructions

WITHOUT DEPENDENT INFINITIVE	WITH DEPENDENT INFINITIVE
Ich **kann** die Aufgabe	Ich **kann** die Aufgabe **lesen**
Ich **konnte** die Aufgabe	Ich **konnte** die Aufgabe **lesen**
Ich **habe** die Aufgabe **gekonnt**	Ich **habe** die Aufgabe **lesen können**
Ich **hatte** die Aufgabe **gekonnt**	Ich **hatte** die Aufgabe **lesen können**
Ich **werde** die Aufgabe **können**	Ich **werde** die Aufgabe **lesen können**
Ich **werde** die Aufgabe **gekonnt haben**	Ich **werde** die Aufgabe **haben lesen können**

a. 1) When no dependent infinitive is expressed in the sentence, the regular past participle with the prefix **ge-** is used (**gekonnt**). 2) When, however, a dependent infinitive is expressed (**lesen**), a past participle without **ge-** is used. This past participle without **ge-** is identical in form with the infinitive of the modal auxiliary (**können**). (See section on word-order, p. 126)

WITH VERBS LIKE: **sehen, hören, helfen, lassen**

Ich habe ihn **arbeiten sehen**	*I saw him work*
Ich habe ihn **sprechen hören**	*I heard him talk*
Ich habe ihr **tragen helfen**	*I helped her carry*
Ich habe ihn **rufen lassen**	*I had him summoned*
Ich habe ihn **gehen lassen**	*I let him go*

b. The same double infinitive construction is optional with verbs like **hören, sehen, helfen,** while always necessary with **lassen.**

A. *Express the meaning of the following sentences in English:*

1. Ich habe meiner Schwester das Paket tragen helfen.
2. Wir haben ihn im Garten sprechen hören.
3. Ich habe die Kinder im Garten spielen sehen.
4. Ich habe den Studenten kommen lassen.
5. Er hat sich die Haare schneiden lassen.

THE VERB

B. *Restate in German:*

1. I have never seen him smoke.
2. We have never heard her sing so well.
3. He had his book printed in Germany. (*lassen*)
4. He left his book (lie) in the classroom. (*lassen*)

C. *Restate in English:*

1. „Durch Erziehung und Beispiel kann man den Menschen das Richtige und Vernüftige, aber man kann ihnen auch das Absurdeste einprägen.“

   (Schopenhauer)

2. „Ein Augenblick der Geduld kann vor großem Unheil bewahren; ein Augenblick der Ungeduld kann ein ganzes Leben zerstören.“

   (Chinesisch)

19 · The Passive Voice

ACTIVE VOICE	Der Student **liest** das Gedicht. Der Student **las** das Gedicht. Der Student **hat** das Gedicht **gelesen.** Der Student **hatte** das Gedicht **gelesen.** Der Student **wird** das Gedicht **lesen.** Der Student **wird** das Gedicht **gelesen haben.**
PASSIVE VOICE	Das Gedicht **wird** von dem Studenten **gelesen.** Das Gedicht **wurde** von dem Studenten **gelesen.** Das Gedicht **ist** von dem Studenten **gelesen worden.** Das Gedicht **war** von dem Studenten **gelesen worden.** Das Gedicht **wird** von dem Studenten **gelesen werden.** Das Gedicht **wird** von dem Studenten **gelesen worden sein.**

a. The passive voice is formed by combining the auxiliary **werden** with the past participle of the verb.*

Das Gedicht	wird wurde ist war wird wird	von dem Studenten	gelesen gelesen gelesen worden gelesen worden gelesen werden gelesen worden sein

b. Note that in the perfect tenses of passive voice (present perfect, past perfect, future perfect) the prefix **ge-** of the past participle of **werden** is dropped, the form **worden** is used.

---

* For complete conjugation of a verb in passive voice see *Synopsis of Grammar*, p. 148.

A. *Complete the following sentences in passive voice:*

1. Karl lernt seine Aufgabe.
    Pres.: Die Aufgabe _____ von Karl _____.
    Pres. Perf.: Die Aufgabe _____ von Karl _____.
    Future: Die Aufgabe _____ von Karl _____.

2. Vater liest die Zeitung.
    Pres.: Die Zeitung _____ von Vater _____.
    Pres. Perf.: Die Zeitung _____ von Vater _____.
    Future: Die Zeitung _____ von Vater _____.

3. Wir verkaufen unser Haus.
    Pres.: Unser Haus _____ von uns _____.
    Pres. Perf.: Unser Haus _____ von uns _____.
    Future: Unser Haus _____ von uns _____.

4. Vater kaufte ein neues Haus.
    Past: Ein neues Haus _____ von Vater _____.

5. Mutter schrieb einen Brief.
    Past: Ein Brief _____ von Mutter _____.

6. Anna hat ihre Schularbeit gut gemacht.
    Pres. Perf.: Die Schularbeit _____ von Anna gut _____.

> *Active:* Unser Lehrer sammelt Gedichte und Volkslieder.
> *Passive:* Gedichte und Volkslieder werden von unserm Lehrer gesammelt.
>
> *Active:* Mein Vater hat die Rechnung bezahlt.
> *Passive:* Die Rechnung ist von meinem Vater bezahlt worden.

c. In changing a sentence from active to passive voice, note: 1) The auxiliary **werden** retains the tense of the active voice. 2) The direct object of the active voice (Gedichte und Volkslieder) becomes the subject of the passive. 3) The subject of the active voice (unser Lehrer) becomes in the passive the agent or the agency (von unserm Lehrer) governed by the preposition **von** or **durch,** English "by".

B. *Restate the following sentences in the passive voice:*

1. Vater hat unser Haus zu billig verkauft.
2. Ein Brand zerstörte unser Rathaus.
3. Wir kamen nach Neapel, und wir hatten das Ziel unserer Reise erreicht.
4. Das Kind war ein Knabe, und sie nannten es nach seinem Vater.
5. Gutenberg erfand die Buchdruckerkunst, und Gutenberg hat den ersten Band der lateinischen Bibel gedruckt.

C. *Change from passive to active voice:*

1. Die Versammlung wurde vom Präsidenten eröffnet.
2. Ein neuer Handelsvertrag ist vom Präsidenten unterzeichnet worden.
3. Der Kongreß wird vom Präsidenten einberufen werden.
4. Ein neuer Richter wurde gestern vom Präsidenten ernannt.
5. Die Steuern sind gestern vom Kongreß herabgesetzt worden.

INSTEAD OF:	IS OFTEN USED:
Das Geld ist ihm geliehen worden.	**Man** hat ihm das Geld geliehen.
Er wurde viel gelobt.	**Man** lobte ihn viel.
Es war mir gesagt worden.	**Man** hatte es mir gesagt.

d. The passive is not as frequent in German as in English. Especially the perfect and future tenses are considered cumbersome. Instead of the passive voice the active with the indefinite pronoun **man** is very common.

D. *Change to active voice and use the indefinite pronoun* **man:**

1. Er ist als berühmter Maler viel geehrt und gefeiert worden.
2. Die Kinder in dieser Familie sind alle gut erzogen worden.
3. Dr. Schmidt starb vor ein paar Tagen, und er ist gestern begraben worden.
4. Die alte Kirche ist abgerissen worden, und mit dem Bau der neuen ist sofort begonnen worden.
5. Hohe Preise sind für die Häuser an dieser Straße gezahlt worden.

20 · The Subjunctive Mood
and the Conditional

I. MEANING OF THE SUBJUNCTIVE

The subjunctive is now rarely used in English. Even in sentences like: *If it were not so cold here, we . . .; If I were you, . . .* the subjunctive form *were* is felt as somewhat formal. The subjunctive has been replaced in large part by the indicative or by word phrases formed with the modal auxiliaries *may, might, could, should, would:*

Would you have time . . .	*We could be back at . . .*
I would suggest that . . .	*We might be home at . . .*

In German similar tendencies are apparent, but they have not advanced so far and subjunctive forms still often occur in everyday speech and are found even more frequently in literature.

While the indicative is the mood of fact and reality, the subjunctive indicates a subjective attitude on the part of the speaker or writer.

II. USE OF THE SUBJUNCTIVE:

1. DESIRE:
Ich möchte gern mitgehen.
I would (should) like to go along.

2. WISH:
Wäre ich nur gesund!
If only I were well!

3. POSSIBILITY:
Das dürfte wahr sein.
It might be true.

4. HESITATION:
Ich hätte wohl das Geld dazu.
I think I would have the money for it.

5. UNCERTAINTY:
Das wäre nicht unmöglich.
That wouldn't be impossible.

6. SOMETHING "CONTRARY TO FACT":
Wenn ich an deiner Stelle gewesen wäre, . . .
If I had been in your place, . . .

a. The subjunctive is used, when the speaker wishes to express or represent something not as a fact or as certain, but as possible, conditional, desirable, or as said or believed by another person.

THE VERB

THE PRESENT SUBJUNCTIVE

haben	werden	reisen	sprechen	tragen	laufen
ich habe	werde	reise	spreche	trage	laufe
du habest	werdest	reisest	sprechest	tragest	laufest
er habe	werde	reise	spreche	trage	laufe
wir haben	werden	reisen	sprechen	tragen	laufen
ihr habet	werdet	reiset	sprechet	traget	laufet
sie haben	werden	reisen	sprechen	tragen	laufen

a. The personal endings of the simple tenses of the subjunctive (present tense and past tense) are: **-e, -est, -e, -en, -et- -en.**

b. Compound tenses of the subjunctive differ from those of the indicative only in that the subjunctive forms of the auxiliaries **haben** and **sein** take the place of their indicative forms.*

THE PAST SUBJUNCTIVE

haben	sein	werden	reisen	sprechen	tragen
ich hätte	wäre	würde	reiste	spräche	trüge
du hättest	wärest	würdest	reistest	sprächest	trügest
er hätte	wäre	würde	reiste	spräche	trüge
wir hätten	wären	würden	reisten	sprächen	trügen
ihr hättet	wäret	würdet	reistet	sprächet	trüget
sie hätten	wären	würden	reisten	sprächen	trügen

c. Umlaut: All three tense auxiliaries, **haben, sein** and **werden,** add umlaut.

d. Strong verbs (**sprechen, tragen, laufen**) add umlaut whenever this is possible (**a - o - u** change to **ä - ö - ü**): **spräche, schlösse, trüge.**

e. The irregular weak verbs **bringen, denken** and **wissen** (see page 20) also add umlaut: **brächte, dächte, wüßte.**

---

* See conjugation of **haben** and **sein,** *Synopsis of Grammar,* pp. 138, 140.

THE VERB

THE SUBJUNCTIVE OF THE MODAL AUXILIARIES

dürfen	können	mögen	sollen	müssen

		PRESENT		
ich dürfe	könne	möge	solle	müsse
du dürfest	könnest	mögest	sollest	müssest
er dürfe	könne	möge	solle	müsse

		PAST		
ich dürfte	könnte	möchte	sollte	müßte
du dürftest	könntest	möchtest	solltest	müßtest
er dürfte	könnte	möchte	sollte	müßte

f. In the present subjunctive the subjunctive endings are added to the stem of the infinitive.

g. In the past subjunctive the modals add to the infinitive stem (as in the present) the regular subjunctive endings plus -t-, retaining the umlaut of the infinitive where it is present.

THE PRESENT SUBJUNCTIVE OF THE VERB sein

Singular:	ich **sei**	du seiest	er **sei**
Plural:	wir seien	ihr seiet	sie seien

h. The personal endings for all tenses of the subjunctive in German are:

Singular: **-e, -est, -t**   Plural: **-en, -et, -en**

The present subjunctive of the verb **sein** offers the sole exception to this rule. There are no endings in the first and third person singular.

IV. MEANING OF THE CONDITIONAL

In addition to the subjunctive forms listed, German has two tense formations called *present conditional* and *past conditional* which occur frequently. They are formed by combining the past subjunctive forms of **werden (ich würde,** etc.) with the present or perfect infinitive of any verb. The conditionals correspond to the use of English *should* and *would*, when the reference is to future time.

In meaning, the two tenses of the conditional are identical with the past and past perfect subjunctives:

Conditional:	Ja, ich würde wohl Zeit haben.
	Yes, I think I would have time.
Subjunctive:	Ja, ich hätte wohl Zeit.
Conditional:	Daran würde ich nie gedacht haben.
	Of that I would never have thought.
Subjunctive:	Daran hätte ich nie gedacht.

The use of the conditional, though often found in literature, is most common in the speech of everyday life.

V. FORMS OF THE CONDITIONAL

THE AUXILIARIES: **haben, sein, werden***

PRESENT CONDITIONAL	PAST CONDITIONAL
I should (would) have	*I should (would) have had*
ich würde haben	ich würde gehabt haben
du würdest haben	du würdest gehabt haben
er würde haben	er würde gehabt haben
wir würden haben	wir würden gehabt haben
ihr würdet haben	ihr würdet gehabt haben
sie würden haben	sie würden gehabt haben
I should (would) be	*I should (would) have been*
ich würde sein	ich würde gewesen sein
du würdest sein	du würdest gewesen sein
er würde sein	er würde gewesen sein
wir würden sein	wir würden gewesen sein
ihr würdet sein	ihr würdet gewesen sein
sie würden sein	sie würden gewesen sein
I should (would) become	*I should (would) have become*
ich würde werden	ich würde geworden sein
du würdest werden	du würdest geworden sein
er würde werden	er würde geworden sein
wir würden werden	wir würden geworden sein
ihr würdet werden	ihr würdet geworden sein
sie würden werden	sie würden geworden sein

---

* For the conjugation of a weak and strong verb see *Synopsis of Grammar,* pp. 144, 146.

21 · Subjunctive and Conditional in Unreal Conditions: Present Time*

CONDITION	CONCLUSION
Wenn ich Zeit **hätte,**	{(so) **käme** ich.** {(so) **würde** ich kommen.
Wenn ich Geld **hätte,**	{(so) **liehe** ich es dir. {(so) **würde** ich es dir leihen.
Wenn ich krank **wäre,** –	{(so) **bliebe** ich zu Hause. {(so) **würde** ich zu Hause bleiben.

The position of the clauses reversed

{Ich **käme,** {Ich **würde** kommen,	wenn ich Zeit **hätte.**
{Ich **liehe** es dir, {Ich **würde** es dir leihen,	wenn ich Geld **hätte.**
{Ich **bliebe** zu Hause, {Ich **würde** zu Hause bleiben,	wenn ich krank **wäre.**

The condition expressed by inversion

Hätte ich Zeit,	{so **käme** ich. {so **würde** ich kommen.
Hätte ich Geld,	{so **liehe** ich es dir. {so **würde** ich es dir leihen.
Wäre ich krank,	{so **bliebe** ich zu Hause. {so **würde** ich zu Hause bleiben.

To express unreal condition **in present time,** German: 1) uses the past subjunctive in both clauses: the condition and the conclusion; or 2) substitutes in the conclusion the present conditional for the past subjunctive.

A. *Change to unreal condition, present time, expressing the conclusion in two ways.*

EXAMPLE: Ich bin krank, ich gehe zum Arzt.
Wenn ich krank **wäre, ginge** ich zum Arzt. (*Subjunctive*)
Wenn ich krank **wäre, würde** ich zum Arzt **gehen.** (*Conditional*)

1. Er ist ein kluger Mann, er tut das nicht.
2. Ich bin müde, ich bleibe zu Hause.

---

* A sentence like "I would come if I had time; **ich käme, wenn ich Zeit hätte**" is called an unreal condition in the present time, because it expresses what would now be if something were now different from actual conditions. The subordinate clause with "if" is called the condition, while the main clause is called the conclusion.
** For the position of **ich** after the main verb, see page 120.

3. Karl hat Geld, er reist nach Deutschland.
4. Du bist hungrig, du ißt.
5. Ich habe Zeit, ich kann die Arbeit machen.
6. Es regnet, ich darf nicht ausgehen.

B. *Substitute in the conclusion of the following sentences the present conditional for the past subjunctive:*

EXAMPLE: Wenn ich das Buch hätte, gäbe ich es dir.
Wenn ich das Buch hätte, **würde** ich es dir **geben.** (*Conditional*)

1. Wenn ich an deiner Stelle wäre, kaufte ich das Haus.
2. Wenn er deutlicher spräche, verständen wir ihn besser.
3. Wenn du den Brief heute schriebest, bekäme er ihn morgen.
4. Wenn ich jetzt Ferien hätte, reiste ich nach dem Süden.

C. *Restate in German, expressing the conclusion in two ways:*

EXAMPLE: If he worked more, he would learn more.
Wenn er mehr arbeitete, **lernte** er mehr. (*Subjunctive*)
Wenn er mehr arbeitete, **würde** er mehr **lernen.** (*Conditional*)

1. If I had the time, I would go to the theater.
2. If it were not so late, I would stay longer.
3. If the nights were cooler, I would sleep better.
4. Even if it were true, would you believe it?
5. If he were your friend, he would not say this.

D. *Change to subjunctive, present time, and reverse the position of the clauses:*

EXAMPLE: Ich bin müde, ich bleibe zu Hause.
Ich **bliebe** zu Hause, wenn ich **müde wäre.** (*Subjunctive*)
Ich **würde** zu Hause **bleiben,** wenn ich **müde wäre.** (*Conditional*)

1. Ich habe Geld, ich bezahle die Rechnung.
2. Ich habe seine Adresse, ich besuche ihn.
3. Er spricht die Wahrheit, ich glaube ihm.
4. Meine Eltern sind alt, sie ziehen nach Florida.
5. Ich weiß die Antwort selber, ich frage dich nicht.

22 · Subjunctive and Conditional in Unreal Conditions: Past Time*

CONDITION	CONCLUSION
Wenn ich Zeit gehabt **hätte,**	(so) **wäre** ich gekommen. (so) **würde** ich gekommen sein.
Wenn ich Geld gehabt **hätte,**	(so) **hätte** ich es dir geliehen. (so) **würde** ich es dir geliehen haben.
Wenn ich krank gewesen **wäre,**	(so) **wäre** ich zu Hause geblieben. (so) **würde** ich zu Hause geblieben sein.

The position of the clauses reversed:

Ich **wäre** gekommen, Ich **würde** gekommen sein,	wenn ich Zeit gehabt **hätte.**
Ich **hätte** es dir geliehen, Ich **würde** es dir geliehen haben,	wenn ich Geld gehabt **hätte.**
Ich **wäre** zu Hause geblieben, Ich **würde** zu Hause geblieben sein,	wenn ich krank gewesen **wäre.**

The condition expressed by inversion:

Hätte ich Zeit gehabt,	so **wäre** ich gekommen. so **würde** ich gekommen sein.
Hätte ich Geld gehabt,	so **hätte** ich es dir geliehen. so **würde** ich es dir geliehen haben.
Wäre ich krank gewesen,	so **wäre** ich zu Hause geblieben. so **würde** ich zu Hause geblieben sein.

To express unreal condition **in past time,** German: 1) uses the past perfect subjunctive in both clauses (the ccndition and the conclusion), or 2) substitutes the past conditional for the past subjunctive in the conclusion.

---

* A sentence like "I would have come if I had had time; **ich wäre gekommen, wenn ich Zeit gehabt hätte"** is called an unreal condition in past time, because it expresses what would have been, if conditions had been different.

A. *Change to unreal condition, past time, expressing the conclusion in two ways:*

EXAMPLE: Ich war krank, ich ging zum Arzt.
Wenn ich krank **gewesen wäre,** (so) **wäre** ich zum Arzt **gegangen.**
(*Subjunctive*)
Wenn ich krank **gewesen wäre,** (so) **würde** ich zum Arzt **gegangen sein.**
(*Conditional*)

1. Ich hatte meine Schularbeit fertig, ich habe sie eingereicht.
2. Wir waren müde, wir wanderten nicht weiter.
3. Das Kleid hat mir gefallen, ich habe es gekauft.
4. Wir gingen früher nach Hause, das Unglück ist nicht geschehen.
5. Du warst zu Hause, ich habe dich besucht.

B. *Omit* **wenn** *and use the past conditional in the conclusion:*

EXAMPLE: Wenn ich müde gewesen wäre, so wäre ich früher nach Hause gegangen.
Wäre ich müde **gewesen,** so **würde** ich früher nach Hause **gegangen sein.** (*Conditional*)

1. Wenn du früher gekommen wärest, so hättest du Marie noch getroffen.
2. Wenn das Bild nicht so teuer gewesen wäre, hätte Vater es gekauft.
3. Wenn wir eine Minute später gekommen wären, hätten wir den Zug verpaßt.
4. Wenn er mir sein Kommen mitgeteilt hätte, so hätte ich ihn mit dem Auto abgeholt.

C. *Restate the following sentences in German:*

EXAMPLE: If I had been in your place, I would not have done that.
Wenn ich an deiner Stelle **gewesen wäre, hätte** ich das nicht **getan.**
(*Subjunctive*)
Wenn ich an deiner Stelle **gewesen wäre, würde** ich das nicht **getan haben.** (*Conditional*)

1. If I had recognized him, I certainly would have spoken to him.
2. If I had known that, I would have brought my friend along.
3. If you had stayed at home, you would not have caught a cold.
4. He certainly would have visited us, if he had been in the city.

D. *Say it in English:*

1. „Wenn wir selber fehlerfrei wären, würde es uns nicht so viel Vergnügen bereiten, Fehler an anderen festzustellen." (Horaz)
2. „Es würde sehr wenig Böses auf Erden getan werden, wenn das Böse nicht immer im Namen des Guten getan werden könnte." (Eschenbach)

23 · Subjunctive in Clauses Introduced by als ob, als wenn

CONDITION	CONCLUSION
Sie sieht aus,	(als ob sie krank **wäre.** (als **wäre** sie krank.
Sie sieht aus,	(als ob sie krank gewesen **wäre.** (als **wäre** sie krank gewesen.
Sie tat,	(als ob sie mich nicht verstanden **hätte.** (als **hätte** sie mich nicht verstanden.

The subjunctive is used in clauses introduced by **als ob** or **als wenn.** If **ob** or **wenn** is omitted, this omission is indicated by placing the finite verb immediately after **als** (inverted word order).*

A. *Restate the following sentences, supplying the correct forms of the verbs indicated:*

> EXAMPLE: Das Kind weinte, als ob ihm das Herz (brechen).
> Das Kind weinte, als ob ihm das Herz **bräche.**

1. Sie tat, als wenn ihr die ganze Welt (gehören).
2. Sie tat, als wenn sie von der ganzen Sache nichts (wissen).
3. Sie tat, als ob sie böse (sein).
4. Er tat, als ob ihn die ganze Sache nichts (angehen).
5. Er lebt, als ob er eine Million (besitzen).
6. Sie sprachen, als wenn sie gern noch länger geblieben (sein).
7. Es sah aus, als wenn wir unser Geld und Haus verlieren (werden).

B. *Restate each of the following sentences with **ob** or **wenn** omitted:*

> EXAMPLE: Es schien, als ob mir die Arbeit nicht gelingen würde.
> Es schien, als würde mir die Arbeit nicht gelingen.

1. Er kam die Straße herauf, als ob er müde oder krank wäre.
2. Er tat, als ob er der ärmste Mensch in der Welt wäre.
3. Die Frau sieht aus, als wenn sie sehr viel gelitten hätte.
4. Der Mann aß, als wenn er seit drei Tagen nichts mehr gegessen hätte.
5. Der Mann erzählte, als wenn er das alles selber gesehen und erlebt hätte.
6. Es schien, als ob wir schlechtes Wetter bekommen würden.
7. Es schneite, als ob es niemals wieder aufhören wollte.

---

* See *Inverted Word Order,* p. 120.

C. *Restate the following sentences in German:*

EXAMPLE: She acted as if she had never seen me before.
Sie tat, **als wenn** sie mich nie vorher gesehen hätte.

1. She looked as if she were tired.
2. He looked as if he had worked hard all day.
3. He spoke as if he were the smartest man in the whole world.
4. He walked as if he were lame or very tired.
5. He spoke as if he had never heard of personal freedom.
6. She acted as if she could not remember.
7. Receive him as if he were your friend.

D. *Say it in English:*

1. „Jeder Tag sollte so gelebt werden, als ob er die Reihe der Tage beende und das Leben restlos erfülle."

(Seneca)

2. „Nichts kränkt den Menschen mehr, als wenn er da, wo er Liebe und Wohlwollen erwarten darf, nicht einmal die geringste Gerechtigkeit findet, und sich eine ungerechte Behandlung gefallen lassen muß."

(Hartmann)

24 · Subjunctive in Clauses Expressing a Wish, Desire or Polite Request

Es **lebe** der König!	*Long live the king!*
Es **lebe** die Freiheit!	*Let freedom ring!*
Gott **segne** dich!	*May God bless you!*

Möge dir diese Arbeit belohnt und dein Wunsch dir erfüllt werden.
May you be rewarded for this work and your wish be fulfilled.
Möge dir auch das neue Jahr nichts als Glück und Freude bringen.
May the New Year bring you nothing but joy and happiness.

a. Chiefly in formal stereotyped phrases, the present subjunctive is used to express a wish conceived as capable of realization.
The present subjunctive of **mögen** with a dependent infinitive may be used in similar meaning.

Hörte er nur auf zu klagen!	
Wenn er nur zu klagen **aufhörte!**	*I wish he would stop*
O, daß er doch zu klagen **aufhörte!**	*complaining.*
Möchte er doch nur zu klagen aufhören!	

b. The past subjunctive, usually accompanied by **doch** or **nur,** is used to express a wish not realized at the present time.

Hätte er nur die Wahrheit **gesprochen!**	
Wenn er nur die Wahrheit **gesprochen hätte!**	*If he only had*
O, daß er nur die Wahrheit **gesprochen hätte!**	*spoken the truth.*

c. The past perfect subjunctive, usually accompanied by **doch** or **nur,** is used to express a wish not realized at a time in the past when its realization would have been desirable.

THE VERB

> **Hätten Sie** für einen Augenblick Zeit für mich?
> *Would you have a moment's time for me?*
> **Dürfte ich** um eine zweite Tasse Kaffee bitten?
> *May I ask for a second cup of coffee?*
> **Würden Sie** bitte morgen nachmittag zum Kaffee zu uns kommen?
> *Would you please come to coffee tomorrow afternoon?*

d. A wish that can and probably will be fulfilled is often expressed in a form of a polite request or question.

A. *Restate in English the following expressions of a wish, desire, or polite request:*

1. Gott gebe es!
2. Gott bewahre!
3. Gott behüte dich!
4. Friede sei mit euch!
5. Glückliche Reise!
6. Gute Besserung!
7. Möge es ihm gelingen!
8. Möge er gesund zurückkommen!
9. Wäre ich nur gesund!
10. Wüßte ich nur, wie er heißt!
11. Wenn er nur Geduld hätte!
12. Wenn ich nur mehr Zeit hätte!
13. Wäre er nur etwas jünger!
14. Arbeitete er nur etwas schneller!
15. Wenn er nur fleißiger gearbeitet hätte!
16. Wenn man ihm nur hätte glauben können!
17. O, daß wir doch seinem Rat gefolgt wären!
18. Wäre er nur mit seinem Auto etwas langsamer gefahren!
19. Dürfte ich Sie um Feuer bitten?
20. Würden Sie mir bitte das Buch leihen?

25 · Subjunctive in Indirect Discourse

The report of a written or spoken statement, thought, or question in a subordinate clause after a verb of saying, thinking, asking, believing, hoping, wishing, or fearing in the main clause is called indirect discourse. The speaker is merely reporting the statement contained in the subordinate clause without assuming any responsibility for the truth of it.

> DIRECT: Karl sagte mir gestern: „Ich habe deinen Vater in New York getroffen."
>
> INDIRECT: Karl sagte mir gestern, er habe meinen Vater in New York getroffen.

MAIN CLAUSE	OBJECT CLAUSE
Er sagte,	daß er kein Geld **habe** (*or* **hätte**).
Er schrieb,	daß er nach Florida **ziehe** (*or* **zöge**).
Ich glaubte,	daß du das Haus gekauft **habest** (*or* **hättest**).
Ich habe gedacht,	daß er uns besuchen **werde** (*or* **würde**).

a. In indirect discourse, if the verb in the main clause is in a tense of the past time (past, present perfect, past perfect) *subjunctive forms are always used in the subordinate clause*, generally retaining the same tense that was or would have been used in direct discourse.

MAIN CLAUSE	OBJECT CLAUSE
Er glaubte,	daß ich das Auto gekauft **hätte.** (*not habe*)
Er dachte,	daß wir nach Deutschland **führen.** (*not* fahren)
Er glaubte,	daß ich all mein Geld verloren **hätte.** (*not habe*)
Ich hoffte,	daß Sie mich einmal besuchen **würden.** (*not werden*)

b. If the present subjunctive form is identical with the indicative form, *the past subjunctive must be used.*

MAIN CLAUSE	OBJECT CLAUSE
Er sagte,	er **bleibe** (*or* **bliebe**) heute zu Hause.
Er schrieb,	er **sei** (*or* **wäre**) krank geworden.
Ich hörte,	er **gehe** (*or* **ginge**) nach Italien.
Ich dachte,	er **werde** (*or* **würde**) nach Deutschland gehen.

c. If the conjunction **daß** is omitted in the subordinate clause, the subordinate clause takes *normal word order.*

MAIN CLAUSE	OBJECT CLAUSE
Er fragte,	ob Vater zu Hause **sei** (*or* **wäre**).
Ich fragte,	ob ich sie begleiten **dürfe** (*or* **dürfte**).
Er fragte,	wo ich das Geld gefunden **hätte**.
Er fragte,	ob ich heute zur Schule **ginge**.

d. Subordinate clauses dependent on verbs of asking are called indirect questions. They are introduced either by **ob** (*whether*) or by an interrogative that functions as a subordinating conjunction, such as **wann, wo, wie,** etc.

A. *Restate the following sentences in indirect discourse, beginning each sentence with:* **Er sagte, daß** . . .

1. Er bleibt heute nachmittag in der Bibliothek und arbeitet.
2. Es ist heute sehr kalt, und ich gehe nicht zur Schule.
3. Er hat den Brief erhalten, er hat ihn aber noch nicht beantwortet.
4. Er ist in Hamburg angekommen und hat auch eine Wohnung gefunden.
5. Sein Bruder studiert in Heidelberg und kommt erst nach zwei Jahren wieder zurück.
6. Das Wetter im Süden ist kalt gewesen, und er ist nach vier Tagen wieder nach Hause gefahren.

THE VERB 51

B. *Restate the following sentences in indirect discourse, beginning each sentence with:* **Er sagte,** ...

1. Er hat kein Geld bei sich und kann die Rechnung nicht bezahlen.
2. Er ist gestern krank gewesen und hat seine Schularbeit nicht gemacht.
3. Ich bin nie zur Schule gegangen und kann weder lesen noch schreiben.
4. Mein Professor spricht sehr schnell und undeutlich, ich kann ihn schlecht verstehen.

C. *Change to indirect discourse: 1) with* **daß,** *2) without* **daß** ...

1. Die Zeitung berichtet: „Das Schiff, die Bremen, ist heute morgen in New York angekommen und hat zweitausend Touristen zurückgebracht.“
2. Er erzählte: „Auf meiner letzten Reise ist mir in einem Hafen in Südamerika mein ganzes Geld gestohlen worden, ich bin für mehrere Tage ganz ohne Mittel gewesen, bis mir meine Bank in New York telegraphisch Geld geschickt hat.“
3. Der Alte erzählte: „Unser Leben in diesem kleinen abgelegenen Dorfe ist zwar etwas einsam aber doch glücklich gewesen. Ich und meine Frau sind von keinen schweren Schicksalsschlägen oder Krankheiten betroffen worden. Wir haben im Leben auch nie Not gelitten. Vor vierzig Jahren sind wir beide als junger Mann und junge Frau in dieses Dorf gekommen. Ich bin als Lehrer hierher berufen worden. Treu und gewissenhaft habe ich alle diese Jahre hindurch als Lehrer gearbeitet. Ich bin von meinen Schülern ebenso geliebt und verehrt worden wie von meinen eigenen Kindern. Meine beiden Kinder sind als Missionare in Afrika tätig. Zwei Enkelkinder sind in unserm Haus. Ihre Eltern haben sie nach Afrika nicht mitnehmen können.“

D. *Restate the following questions as indirect questions, starting each sentence:* **Man fragte mich,** ...

1. Wie heißen Sie?
2. Wo wohnen Sie in dieser Stadt?
3. Wann sind Sie geboren?
4. Wo haben Sie zuletzt gearbeitet?
5. Wovon leben Sie jetzt?
6. Sind Sie verheiratet?
7. Sind Sie schon einmal gerichtlich bestraft worden?
8. Warum sind Sie letzte Nacht bei Herrn Schmidt eingebrochen?
9. Warum haben Sie von dem Gelde nur einen Dollar genommen und das andere Geld liegen lassen?

E. *Restate the following sentences as indirect questions, starting each sentence:* **Man fragte, ob . . .**

1. Sind deine Eltern von ihrer Europareise schon zurückgekommen?
2. Bist du krank, oder bist du krank gewesen?
3. Ich habe das Auto gekauft und die ganze Kaufsumme sofort bezahlt.
4. Mein Bruder Karl ist ein berühmter Maler geworden und hat schon viele Bilder verkauft.
5. Ich habe meine Studien in Deutschland beendet und fahre nun nach Amerika zurück.

26 · Indirect Discourse With Indicative

MAIN CLAUSE	OBJECT CLAUSE
Ich weiß,	daß er zu Hause **ist**.
Wir hoffen,	daß du das Geld **hast**.
Ich fürchte,	daß er nicht kommen **wird**.
Ich sage dir,	daß es unmöglich **ist**.
Er denkt,	daß alles verloren **ist**.
Er fragt,	ob Vater zu Hause **ist**.
Ich weiß bestimmt,	daß du Unrecht **hast**.
Ich sehe,	daß du sehr müde **bist**.
Es ist klar,	daß er heute nicht kommen **kann**.
Es ist nicht zu leugnen,	daß er ein großer Künstler **ist**.
Das beweist,	was du tun **kannst**.

In indirect discourse: 1) If the verb in the main clause is in the present tense, indicative forms are generally used in the object clause.* 2) Indicative forms are also used after verbs such as **wissen** (*to know*), **sehen** (*to see*), **beweisen** (*to prove*), and phrases such as **es ist klar** (*it is clear*), **es ist nicht zu leugnen** (*it cannot be denied*).**

A. *Restate the following sentences in English:*

1. Ich weiß, daß er in München studiert hat.
2. Ich fürchte, daß ich diese Arbeit nicht fertigmachen kann.
3. Sie schreibt, daß sie heute abend nicht kommen kann.
4. Sie sagt, daß sie nicht mehr zur Schule gehen will.
5. Er fragt, ob du Lehrer werden willst.
6. Ich glaube nicht, daß er sich für fremde Sprachen interessiert.
7. Ich bin überzeugt, daß er viel älter ist, als er sagt.
8. Es ist klar, daß er ein großer Künstler ist.
9. Es ist nicht zu leugnen, daß er ein begabter Mensch ist.
10. Das beweist, daß er arbeiten kann, wenn er will.

---

* The use of the present tense in the main clause, especially with verbs of knowing, asking, proving, etc., emphasizes, supports, or endorses the truth of what follows; consequently, the indicative, *as the mood of fact*, is used to express this certainty.
** It should be mentioned that in the writings of many modern German authors there is a definite tendency to replace the subjunctive in indirect discourse by the indicative.

B. *Restate the following sentences in German:*

1. I tell you and you can believe me that this man is innocent.
2. He writes that he has lost all his (*sein ganzes*) money.
3. That proves that he is interested in (*sich interessiert für*) music.
4. It can not be denied that he is a great artist.
5. It is clear that he is not telling the truth.
6. I know that he works hard and has to pass (*bestehen*) his examinations.
7. I don't doubt that Karl will be a successful businessman in a few years.
8. We believe that he is the most influential (*einflußreichste*) man in this town.
9. The newspaper reports that they had a severe snowstorm in the East.
10. I suspect (*vermuten*) he is lying and is trying to deceive us.

C. *Restate in English:*

1. Er versichert (*assures*), er hat den Diebstahl nicht begangen und ist gestern den ganzen Abend zu Hause gewesen.
2. Er behauptet (*asserts*), Karl hat das Auto genommen und hat es ohne sein Wissen gefahren.
3. Der Zeuge sagt aus (*testifies*), er hat Karl mit dem Auto die Straße hinabfahren sehen.
4. Er leugnet (*denies*), daß er die Kontrolle über das Auto verloren hat.
5. Er versichert (*assures*), daß er das Auto nicht hat stehlen und verkaufen wollen.
6. Man sagt, (*people say*), Karl ist immer ein leichtsinniger und unzuverlässiger junger Mann gewesen.
7. Ich weiß nicht warum, aber diese Frau gibt vor (*pretends*), sie kennt mich nicht und hat mich nie gesehen.
8. Wir vermuten (*suspect*), daß Marie sich mit Karl verheiraten wird.

THE NOUN

1 · Gender, Number, and Case of Nouns

	MASCULINE	FEMININE	NEUTER
	SINGULAR		
Nominative	der Lehrer	die Straße	das Bild
Genitive	des Lehrers	der Straße	des Bildes
Dative	dem Lehrer	der Straße	dem Bild
Accusative	den Lehrer	die Straße	das Bild
	PLURAL		
Nominative	die Lehrer	die Straßen	die Bilder
Genitive	der Lehrer	der Straßen	der Bilder
Dative	den Lehrern	den Straßen	den Bildern
Accusative	die Lehrer	die Straßen	die Bilder

A German noun has 1) **gender:** masculine, feminine, neuter; 2) **number:** singular, plural; 3) **case:** nominative, genitive, dative, accusative.

A. *Follow the model* **der Lehrer** *and decline the following nouns in singular and plural:*

der Winter, der Diener, der Wagen, der Morgen, der Onkel, der Flügel

B. *Follow the model* **die Straße** *and decline the following nouns in singular and plural:*

die Schule, die Frage, die Blume, die Pflanze

C. *Follow the model* **das Bild** *and decline the following nouns in singular and plural:*

das Feld, das Kind, das Licht, das Gesicht

D. *In the following phrases give gender, number and case of the nouns.*

EXAMPLE: Die Arbeiten   meiner Schüler   in den letzten Tagen
       Fem. Plural, Nom.   *Masc. Plural, Gen.*   *Masc. Plural, Dat.*

1. Die Kinder in den Schulen der Stadt.
2. Die Bilder an den Wänden in meinem Zimmer.
3. Die Wohnung des Lehrers neben der Kirche.
4. Die Winter in diesem Lande in den letzten Jahren waren sehr kalt.
5. Die Schule ist im Sommer geschlossen, die Kinder haben Ferien.

2 · Strong Declension of Nouns

	MASCULINE	FEMININE	NEUTER
		SINGULAR	
N.	der Bruder	die Nacht	das Haus
G.	des Bruders	der Nacht	des Hauses
D.	dem Bruder	der Nacht	dem Haus
A.	den Bruder	die Nacht	das Haus
		PLURAL	
N.	die Brüder	die Nächte	die Häuser
G.	der Brüder	der Nächte	der Häuser
D.	den Brüdern	den Nächten	den Häusern
A.	die Brüder	die Nächte	die Häuser

Strong Declension. *Singular:* 1) feminine nouns remain unchanged; 2) masculine and neuter nouns add -s or -es to the nominative singular to form the genitive. *Plural:* masculine, feminine, and neuter nouns have either: 1) no ending, except -n in the dative; 2) the ending -e, plus -n in the dative; or 3) the ending -er, plus -n in the dative.*

A. *Decline the following nouns, belonging to the strong declension, in both singular and plural (for vowel-changes and plural endings consult the vocabulary):*

1. der Vater, der Apfel, der Garten; die Mutter, die Tochter; das Fenster das Mädchen.
2. der Baum, der Sohn; die Bank, die Stadt; das Jahr, das Haar.
3. der Mann, der Wald; das Land, das Dorf.

B. *Give the genitive and accusative singular and the nominative and dative plural of the following nouns:*

1. der Nagel, der Hammer, der Ofen
2. der Herbst, die Hand, das Brot
3. das Buch, das Glas, das Gras

C. *Restate in the plural:*

1. Der Lehrer fragt, und der Schüler antwortet.
2. Die Mutter arbeitet, und die Tochter spielt.
3. Der Bürger lebt in der Stadt und der Mann in dem Dorf.
4. Das Glas zersprang in meiner Hand.

---

* See *Synopsis of Grammar*, p. 160.

3 · Weak Declension of Nouns

MASCULINE
      FEMININE

		SINGULAR		
N.	der Soldat	der Mensch	die Welt	die Lehrerin
G.	des Soldaten	des Menschen	der Welt	der Lehrerin
D.	dem Soldaten	dem Menschen	der Welt	der Lehrerin
A.	den Soldaten	den Menschen	die Welt	die Lehrerin
		PLURAL		
N.	die Soldaten	die Menschen	die Welten	die Lehrerinnen
G.	der Soldaten	der Menschen	der Welten	der Lehrerinnen
D.	den Soldaten	den Menschen	den Welten	den Lehrerinnen
A.	die Soldaten	die Menschen	die Welten	die Lehrerinnen

Weak Declension. *Singular:* 1) feminine nouns remain unchanged; 2) masculine nouns add -n or -en to the nominative to form all other singular cases. *Plural:* masculine and feminine nouns add -n or -en to the nominative singular to form all plural cases.*

A. *Decline the following nouns, belonging to the weak declension, in both singular and plural:*

1. der Student, der Junge, der Löwe, der Polizist
2. die Frau, die Zeit, die Freundin, die Königin

B. *Give the genitive and the accusative singular and the nominative and dative plural of the following nouns:*

1. der Knabe, der Geselle, der Hirte, der Prophet
2. die Zahl, die Ecke, die Nachbarin, die Schülerin

C. *Restate in the plural:*

1. Der Student verließ die Universität und wurde Soldat.
2. Ich kann die Antwort auf diese Frage nicht finden.
3. Der Hirte hütete die Herde.

D. *Restate in the singular:*

1. Diese Jungen sind meine Freunde.
2. Wir sahen die Frauen in ihren Gärten arbeiten.
3. Sie sprach von ihren Lehrerinnen und Freundinnen.

---

* See *Synopsis of Grammar*, p. 162.

     THE NOUN

4 · Mixed Declension of Nouns

	MASCULINE			NEUTER
	SINGULAR			
N.	der Schmerz	der Nachbar	der Doktor	das Auge
G.	des Schmerzes	des Nachbars	des Doktors	des Auges
D.	dem Schmerz	dem Nachbar	dem Doktor	dem Auge
A.	den Schmerz	den Nachbar	den Doktor	das Auge
	PLURAL			
N.	die Schmerzen	die Nachbarn	die Doktoren	die Augen
G.	der Schmerzen	der Nachbarn	der Doktoren	der Augen
D.	den Schmerzen	den Nachbarn	den Doktoren	den Augen
A.	die Schmerzen	die Nachbarn	die Doktoren	die Augen

A few masculine and neuter nouns are strong in the singular and weak in the plural.*

A. *Decline the following nouns in both singular and plural:*

1. der Bauer, der See (*pl.* Se-en), der Staat, der Professor
2. das Ende, das Ohr, das Bett

B. *Give the genitive and the accusative singular and the nominative plural of the following nouns:*

der Direktor, der Inspektor, der Senator, der Rektor, der Autor

C. *Rewrite the following phrases in the plural:*

1. der Regent des Staates
2. der Doktor dieses Kranken
3. das Haus des Nachbars
4. der Direktor der Schule
5. der See in diesem Lande
6. die Mutter mit ihrer Tochter
7. der Bruder des Professors
8. der Bauer und die Bäuerin

D. *Rewrite the following phrases in the singular:*

1. die Augen dieser Knaben
2. die Schmerzen in meinen Ohren
3. die Inspektoren der Automobile
4. die Brüder mit den Schwestern
5. die Schneider und die Schneiderinnen
6. Diese Männer sind Professoren, jene Männer sind Doktoren.

---

* See *Synopsis of Grammar*, p. 162.

5 · Irregular Nouns

	MASCULINE		NEUTER	
		SINGULAR		
N.	{der Name / der Namen	der Gedanke	der Herr	das Herz
G.	des Namens	des Gedankens	des Herrn	des Herzens
D.	dem Namen	dem Gedanken	dem Herrn	dem Herzen
A.	den Namen	den Gedanken	den Herrn	das Herz
		PLURAL		
N.	die Namen	die Gedanken	die Herren	die Herzen
G.	der Namen	der Gedanken	der Herren	der Herzen
D.	den Namen	den Gedanken	den Herren	den Herzen
A.	die Namen	die Gedanken	die Herren	die Herzen

A few masculine nouns have a nominative singular in both -e and -en: **der Name** or **der Namen, der Gedanke** or **der Gedanken, der Same** or **der Samen.** They are declined strong with no endings in the plural. The neuter noun, **das Herz,** does not have the ending **-en** in the nominative and accusative singular.*

A. *Decline the following nouns in both singular and plural:*

der Wille, der Funke

B. *Decline the following nouns in singular* (*plural rarely used*):

der Glaube, der Friede

C. *Change all the nouns in the following expressions from the singular to the plural:*

1. der Name des Lehrers
2. der Gedanke des Studenten
3. der Same der Pflanze
4. das Herz der Mutter
5. der Funke im Feuer
6. die Arbeit des Schülers
7. das Werk des Dichters
8. der Name der Stadt
9. die Mutter des Mädchens
10. die Freundin meiner Schwester

D. *Change all the nouns from the plural to singular:*

1. die Arbeiten unserer Lehrer
2. die Samen der Pflanzen
3. die Gedanken unseres Vaters
4. die Herzen der Kinder
5. die Namen der Dichter
6. die Frieden von Versailles

---

* See *Synopsis of Grammar*, p. 163.

THE NOUN

6 · Principal Parts of Nouns

NOMINATIVE SINGULAR	GENITIVE SINGULAR	NOMINATIVE PLURAL
der Wagen	des Wagens	die Wagen
der Baum	des Baumes	die Bäume
das Blatt	des Blattes	die Blätter
die Taube	der Taube	die Tauben
der Knabe	des Knaben	die Knaben

The principal parts of a noun are those key-forms from which all other forms may be derived. They are: the nominative and genitive singular and the nominative plural.

A. *Give the principal parts of the following nouns (for plural endings and umlaut consult the vocabulary):*

1. der Schlüssel   die Stadt   das Feld   die Straße   der Nachbar
2. die Tochter   die Nacht   das Lied   die Seite   das Auge
3. das Mädchen   das Gedicht das Volk   die Rose   das Ende
4. der Vogel   der Mann   der Wald   der Junge   das Herz

B. *Give the principal parts of the nouns in the following reading selection:*

Die Frau wohnte in einer stillen Straße nahe der Stadtmauer. Die Frau war eine Witwe, ihr Mann war vor einem Jahr gestorben. Ihr Mann hatte ihr ein kleines Haus, ein paar Acker Land und zwei Kinder, einen Sohn und eine Tochter, hinterlassen. Der Sohn war ein Knabe mit grauen Augen und einem ernsten Gesicht. Seine Schwester war ein Mädchen von zwölf Jahren. Es war ein schönes Kind mit braunem Haar, braunen Augen und weißer Hautfarbe.

C. *Restate the following in German:*

1. the days of the week
2. the months of the year
3. books for children
4. the flowers in the gardens
5. the children in our schools
6. the farmers in the country
7. questions and answers
8. (My) Ladies and gentlemen.
9. A (*Das*) year has fifty-two weeks and one day.
10. Our neighbor has two daughters and three sons.
11. Its cold here, my hands and my feet are cold.
12. Men, women and children are working in (*auf*) the fields.

7 · Compound Nouns

NOUN	NOUN	COMPOUND
der Wald	die Blume	**die Waldblume**
die Schule	das Mädchen	**das Schulmädchen**
das Haus	die Frau	**die Hausfrau**
das Tier	der Arzt	**der Tierarzt**

a. The last part of a compound noun determines its gender and declension. The main accent rests on the first compound part.

A. *Form compound nouns of the following pairs of nouns. Give the meaning of the nouns and of their compounds:*

1. der Winter / der Tag
2. die Augen / der Arzt
3. die Schule / das Geld
4. die Kinder / der Garten
5. die Schule / das Mädchen
6. das Mädchen / die Schule
7. das Feld / die Arbeit
8. der Apfel / der Baum
9. die Wörter / das Buch
10. die Blumen / der Garten
11. die Tannen / der Wald
12. das Fenster / die Scheibe

B. *Give the meaning of the following compound nouns and of each of their component parts:*

1. das Bilderbuch
2. die Straßenecke
3. der Obstbaum
4. der Reisewagen

das Wirtshaus
die Tageszeitung
der Todfeind
der Frühlingsmorgen

das Volkslied
die Jahreszeiten
der Geburtstag
der Geographielehrer

C. *Give the principal parts of the following nouns:*

1. das Volkslied
2. das Geschäftshaus
3. der Bürgermeister
4. die Seitenstraße

die Jahreszeit
die Briefmarke
die Liedersammlung
der Familienname

der Geburtstag
der Sommermonat
das Bilderbuch
der Bauinspektor

der Kaufmann, *merchant*, die Kaufleute
der Fuhrmann, *driver (of a wagon)*, die Fuhrleute
der Landmann, *peasant*, die Landleute

b. Certain compound nouns, ending in **-mann**, take **-leute** in plural.*

* BUT: der Ehemann, die **Ehemänner**; der Ehrenmann, die **Ehrenmänner**; der Staatsmann, die **Staatsmänner**

A. *Give the plural of the following compound nouns:*

1. der Edelmann, *nobleman;*   der Hauptmann, *captain;*
   der Seemann, *sailor;*
2. der Bauersmann, *farmer;*   der Geschäftsmann, *businessman;*
   der Handelsmann, *tradesman;*
3. der Handwerksmann, *artisan;*   der Landsmann, *compatriot;*
   der Hofmann, *courtier*

B. *Say it in English:*

1. Fuhrleute bringen Waren für unsere Geschäftsleute in die Stadt.
2. Edelleute waren nicht immer Ehrenmänner.
3. Hauptleute führen eine Kompanie Soldaten.
4. Geschäftsleute und Handelsleute gründeten eine Handelsgesellschaft in unserer Stadt.

C. *Say it in English:*

1. Bedenken Sie (*bear in mind*), Pläne sind noch keine Entschlüsse, und Vorsätze sind noch keine Grundsätze.
2. Kennen Sie die Werke der Professoren Max Hartung und Ernst Fries über den Ursprung des Menschengeschlechts? Doktoren und Professoren streiten immer noch über diese Frage.
3. Singt eure Lieder, spielt eure Spiele, Kinder, malt eure Bilder, lernt von euren Eltern und Lehrern und lest die Bücher eurer Dichter und Denker!

8 · The Accusative Case as Direct Object

SUBJECT	DIRECT OBJECT
Der Lehrer fragt	**den Schüler.**
Er fragt	**einen Schüler.**
Der Schüler schreibt	**die Aufgabe.**
Er schreibt	**eine Aufgabe.**
Der Lehrer liest	**das Gedicht.**
Der Schüler lernt	**das Gedicht.**
Er lernt	**ein Gedicht.**

The accusative case is used as direct object of transitive verbs. It corresponds to the objective case in English.

A. *In the following sentences indicate: 1) each subject (S); 2) each direct object (O):*

1. Ich habe diese deutsche Novelle noch nicht gelesen.
2. Meine Studenten haben Goethes *Hermann und Dorothea* noch nicht gelesen.
3. Dieses Gedicht hat Goethe nicht geschrieben.
4. Haben Sie mit ihren Schülern einige Balladen von Schiller gelesen?
5. Haben Sie auf ihrer Deutschlandreise auch die Stadt Köln besucht?
6. Dieses Buch habe ich aus unserer Stadtbibliothek entliehen.

B. *Restate the following sentences in German and list the direct object in each sentence*

1. The children were visiting their grandparents.
2. We'll read this German play next semester.
3. Didn't you see the boy who broke the window?
4. Yesterday she wrote her first poem.
5. I saw our new teacher yesterday for the first time.
6. Why don't you answer my question?

C. *In the following sentences, note the double accusative object. Restate the sentences in English:*

1. Alle Welt nennt ihn einen Narren.
2. Wir nennen sie unsere beste Lehrerin.
3. Den Monat Mai heißen wir den Frühlingsmonat.
4. Wer hat dich Latein gelehrt?
5. Die Klugheit lehrt mich Verschwiegenheit.

9 · The Accusative After Certain Prepositions

	PREPOSITION	ACCUSATIVE
Unser Weg führte	**durch**	den Wald.
Ich kaufte das Buch	**für**	meinen Freund.
Er fuhr sein Auto	**gegen**	die Hausecke.
Er kam zur Schule	**ohne**	seine Schularbeit.
Er bat uns alle	**um**	Hilfe.

The following prepositions always govern the accusative case: **durch,** *through;* **für,** *for;* **gegen** or **wider,** *against, contrary to;* **ohne,** *without;* **um,** *about, around.*

A. *Restate the following sentences, supplying the correct forms of the missing definite and indefinite articles:*

1. Die Kinder liefen durch _____ Haus, durch _____ Garten auf die Straße.
2. Er schrieb das Gedicht für _____ Lehrer, für _____ Lehrerin.
3. Das Kind lief mit der Stirn gegen _____ Tür, gegen _____ Baum.
4. Sie kam zur Schule ohne _____ Buch, ohne _____ Füllfeder.
5. Der Weg führte um _____ Stadt, um _____ See (herum).
6. Er handelt wider _____ Regel, wider _____ Verabredung.

B. *Restate the following sentences, supplying the correct missing accusative endings:*

1. Ohne mein_ Hilfe ist er verloren.
2. Du kannst nicht gegen d_ Strom schwimmen.
3. Ich habe ein Geschenk für mein_ kleine Schwester gekauft.
4. Du handelst wider unser_ Verabredung.
5. Was hast du gegen dies_ Kind?
6. Du kämpfst gegen ein_ stärkeren Gegner.
7. Er ging um d_ Haus herum.
8. Er zeigte ein Lächeln um sein_ Mund.
9. Der Stein flog gegen sein_ Stirn.
10. Er verlor seine Stellung durch sein_ eigene Schuld.

10 · The Accusative in Phrases Answering Wohin?

	PREPOSITION	ACCUSATIVE
Der Lehrer kommt	**in**	das Zimmer.
Er geht	**an**	den Tisch.
Er legt sein Buch	**auf**	den Tisch.
Er stellt den Stuhl	**hinter**	den Tisch.
Er tritt	**vor**	die Klasse.

In phrases in which motion towards a place is expressed, the accusative case follows the prepositions: **an,** *at, to, up against;* **auf,** *on, upon, for, to;* **hinter,** *behind;* **in,** *in, into;* **neben,** *beside;* **über,** *above, over, across, about;* **unter,** *under, among;* **vor,** *before, in front of;* **zwischen,** *between.* The accusative answers the German question **wohin?** *to what place? whither?*

A. *Restate the following sentences, supplying the correct forms of the missing endings:*

1. Er hängt das Bild an d_ Wand, über d_ Wandtafel.
2. Die Kinder laufen in d_ Garten, hinter d_ Haus.
3. Im nächsten Jahr ziehen wir in d_ Stadt.
4. Wir bauen unser Haus rechts neben d_ Kirche.
5. Karl geht in d_ Schule, er setzt sich neben d_ kleinen Ernst.
6. Er setzt sich zwischen mein_ Bruder und mein_ Schwester.
7. Er schreibt seinen Namen in d_ Buch und legt das Buch auf d_ Tisch.
8. Er stellt den Papierkorb unter d_ Tisch.
9. Er steckt das Geld in sein_ Tasche.
10. Das Kind ging an d_ See und fiel in d_ Wasser.
11. Bitte, schreiben Sie Ihre Adresse auf d_ Briefumschlag.
12. Stecken Sie den Brief in d_ Briefkasten.

B. *Restate the following sentences in German:*

1. He is going to the blackboard.
2. He puts (*legen*) his homework on the table.
3. He set down (*sich setzen*) beside his friend Karl.
4. He swam across the lake.
5. Carry the package into the house.
6. Take (*bringen*) this letter to (*auf*) the post office.
7. Mother went to (*auf*) the market.
8. Don't put your overcoat on a chair, hang it in the closet.
9. They rowed across the lake.
10. He put (*stecken*) a ring on her finger.

C. *Restate the following sentences in English:*

1. Wir hoffen und warten auf (*for*) besseres Wetter.
2. Wir sind nur auf (*for a*) kurze Zeit hier.
3. Bitte, sagen Sie das auf (*in*) deutsch.
4. Wir sind stolz auf (*proud of*) unsere Tochter.
5. Er steckte das Geld in (*into*) seine Tasche.
6. Er brachte Sorgen und Elend über (*over*) das Land.

11 · The Dative Case as the Indirect Object

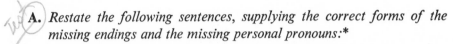

	INDIRECT OBJECT	DIRECT OBJECT
Der Schüler zeigt	**dem Lehrer**	seine Arbeit.
Er schreibt	**der Mutter**	einen Brief.
Er gibt	**dem Kind**	ein Geschenk.
Er zeigt	**mir**	seine Füllfeder.
Ich gebe	**dir**	mein Messer.
Er kauft	**ihm**	eine Uhr.

The dative case is used to express the indirect object.

A. *Restate the following sentences, supplying the correct forms of the missing endings and the missing personal pronouns:**

1. Karl schenkt d_ Schwester eine neue Füllfeder. Er schenkt (*her*) eine neue Füllfeder.
2. Karl bringt sein_ Lehrer Blumen zum Geburtstag. Er bringt (*him*) Blumen zum Geburtstag.
3. Karl zeigt sein_ Freundin, Marie, die neue Bibliothek. Er zeigt (*her*) die neue Bibliothek.
4. Vater kauft sein_ Tochter eine goldene Uhr. Er kauft (*her*) eine goldene Uhr.
5. Sage d_ Mann deinen Namen und deine Adresse. Sage (*him*) deinen Namen und deine Adresse.
6. Der Arzt macht d_ Kranken gute Hoffnung. Der Arzt macht (*him*) gute Hoffnung.
7. Der Briefträger bringt unser_ Vater einen Brief. Er bringt (*him*) einen Brief.
8. Die Aufregung schadet d_ Kranken. Die Aufregung schadet (*him*).
9. Dieses Armband gehört mein_ Mutter. Dieses Armband gehört (*her*).

B. *Restate the following sentences, expressing the direct object by a personal pronoun (watch the word order):*

1. Schenken Sie mir das Bild.
2. Bringe deinem Vater die Zeitung.
3. Sagen Sie mir ihren Namen.
4. Ich habe ihm seine Briefe zurückgegeben.
5. Ich bringe Ihnen die geliehenen Bücher zurück.
6. Vater hat mir diese goldene Uhr zum Geburtstag geschenkt.

* See section on personal pronouns, page 104.

THE NOUN

12 · The Dative of Sole Object

	VERB	OBJECT
Der Arzt	hilft	**dem Kranken.**
Das Geld	gehört	**meinem Vater**
Das Kind	folgt	**seinen Eltern.**

The dative case is used as sole object after certain verbs. The most common verbs, taking the dative case, are: **antworten,** to answer; **begegnen,** to meet; **danken,** to thank; **dienen,** to serve; **drohen,** to threaten; **folgen,** to follow, to obey; **gehören,** to belong to; **gelingen,** to succeed; **glauben,** to believe; **helfen,** to help; **sich nähern,** to approach; **schaden,** to harm, hurt.

A. *Restate the following sentences in German:*

1. I do not believe the man. I do not believe him.
2. She helps mother. She helps her.
3. I help father. I help him.
4. The dog does not obey his master. It does not obey him.
5. Our class obeys the teacher. It obeys her.
6. This money does not belong to me. It belongs to her.
7. The student does not succeed (*gelingen*) in his work.
8. I do not succeed in my work.
9. He has served his master faithfully. He has served him.
10. You have served your country faithfully.
11. I have served our country faithfully.
12. We met the stranger on the street (*begegnen*). We met him.
13. We followed him into the house. We followed the man into the house.
14. This bracelet belongs to my mother. It belongs to her.
15. Be careful! That will harm your health. It will harm you.

B. *Answer the following questions:*

> EXAMPLE: Wem hilft die Tochter? (die Mutter)
> Die Tochter hilft **der Mutter.**

1. Wem dient der Bürgermeister? (die Stadt)
2. Wem dient der Beamte? (der Staat)
3. Wem gehorchen die Kinder? (die Eltern)
4. Wem folgt der Hund? (sein Herr)
5. Wem antwortet das Schulkind? (seine Lehrerin)
6. Wem hilft die Medizin? (der Kranke)
7. Wem dankt der Kranke? (der Arzt)

13 · The Dative After Certain Prepositions

	PREPOSITION	DATIVE
Die Leute kommen	**aus**	dem Theater.
Dieser Garten gehört	**zu**	dem Haus.
Der Student wohnt	**bei**	seinem Bruder.
Was denken Sie	**von**	dieser Geschichte?

The following prepositions always govern the dative: **aus,** *from, out of;* **bei,** *by, at, near, at the home of;* **mit,** *with;* **nach,** *to, for, after, toward, according to;* **seit,** *since;* **von,** *of, from, about;* **zu,** *to, at.*

A. *Restate the following sentences, supplying the correct forms of the definite article:*

1. Ich komme aus ____ Stadt, aus ____ Schule, aus ____ Theater, aus ____ Vorlesung.
2. Karl wohnt bei ____ Mutter, bei ____ Herrn Schmidt, bei ____ Großeltern.
3. Ich sprach gestern mit ____ Professor, mit ____ Lehrerin, mit ____ Kindern, mit ____ Eltern der Kinder.
4. Es war nach ____ Kriege, nach ____ Studienzeit, nach ____ Tode seiner Mutter, er besuchte uns nach ____ Abendessen.

B. *Restate the following phrases and sentences in English:*

1. Er kommt aus (*from*) Deutschland, aus Frankreich, aus England.
2. Es ist eine Zeile aus (*from a*) einem Gedicht, aus einem Drama.
3. Sie kam aus (*from*) der Kirche, aus dem Theater.
4. Ich weiß das aus (*from*) Erfahrung. Es war ein Märchen aus (*of*) alten Zeiten.
5. Wir riefen ihn bei (*by*) seinem Namen. Er wohnte bei (*with*) meinem Bruder.
6. Er wohnt bei (*with*) uns, er bleibt bei (*with*) mir. Ich nehme ihn bei (*at his*) seinem Wort.
7. Er arbeitet mit (*with*) gutem Erfolg. Er arbeitet mit (*with*) großem Fleiß.
8. Ich reise von (*from*) Frankfurt nach (*to*) Berlin. Karl ist von Geburt (*by birth*) ein Deutscher.

C. *Restate in English:*

1. „Erst zweifeln, dann untersuchen, dann entdecken. Der Zweifel führt zum Forschen, das Forschen führt zum Fortschritt, zum Entdecken, zum Wissen."
   (Henry Th. Buckle)

14 · The Dative in Phrases Answering <u>Wo</u>?

Das Auto steht	vor	dem Haus.
Sonnenschein liegt	über	der Stadt.
Mein Freund sitzt	neben	mir.
Dein Vater steht	hinter	dir.

When the verb in the sentence denotes locality or position, the dative case follows the prepositions: **an, auf, hinter, in, neben, über, unter, vor, zwischen.** The dative answers the German question **wo?** *where?*

A. *Restate the following sentences, supplying the correct forms of the definite article:*

1. Der Student steht an _____ Wandtafel, an _____ Tür, wartet an _____ Straßenecke, denkt an _____ Ferien.
2. Sein Buch liegt auf _____ Tisch, auf _____ Bank, auf _____ Fußboden.
3. Der Garten liegt hinter _____ Haus, ein See liegt hinter _____ Bergen. –
4. Die Kinder sind in _____ Schule, Mutter ist in _____ Küche, Vater ist in _____ Stadt.
5. Nebel lag über den Feldern, Dunkelheit lag über _____ Erde, der Mond stand über _____ Bäumen.
6. Die Freundschaft zwischen _____ Kantor und _____ Lehrer wurde zu einer dauernden Freundschaft.
7. Es ist ein großer Unterschied zwischen _____ Gefährten und _____ Freunden.

B. *Restate the following sentences, supplying the correct forms of the missing endings:*

1. Ich hörte ihn in sein_ Zimmer auf und ab gehen.
2. Er studiert hier auf unser_ Universität und arbeitet viel in d_ Bibliothek.
3. Er sitzt an mein_ Seite zwischen mir und d_ Fräulein Klein.
4. Ich begegnete ihm auf d_ Marktplatz, auf mein_ Wege zur Vorlesung in d_ Universität.
5. Vater baut uns ein Haus auf ein_ Anhöhe vor unser_ Stadt.
6. Die kleine Stadt liegt an ein_ kleinen Fluß an d_ Küste Schottlands.
7. Wie stehen die Sachen zwischen Ihn_ und Ihr_ Nachbarn?
8. Ich fand den Brief zwischen d_ Blättern eines alten Buches.

C. *Restate the following phrases and sentences in German:*

1. At daylight; at night; at one end.
2. At the foot of a mountain.
3. At the head (*die Spitze*) of a great army.
4. What have you in your hand?
5. We were standing at the window.
6. The city of Bonn lies on the river Rhein.
7. I'll show you the city on the map.
8. It was ten degrees below the freezing-point.
9. He has no respect for the law.
10. Schiller's letters to (*an*) Goethe.

NOTE

Many prepositions form contractions with the dative and accusative of the definite article:

im	= **in dem**	: im Garten, im Dorf, im Frühling
ins	= **in das**	: ins Wasser, ins Konzert, ins Geschäft
am	= **an dem**	: am Arm, am Fluß, am Bach
ans	= **an das**	: ans Ufer, ans Wasser, ans Schiff
aufs	= **auf das**	: aufs Feld, aufs Land, aufs Dach
fürs	= **für das**	: fürs Geld, fürs Kind, fürs Haus
übers	= **über das**	: übers Haus, übers Feuer, übers Jahr
vom	= **von dem**	: vom Feld, vom Himmel, vom Vater
beim	= **bei dem**	: beim Arzt, beim Spiel, beim Essen
zum	= **zu dem**	: zum Herrn, zum Glück, zum Beispiel
zur	= **zu der**	: zur Stadt, zur Schule, zur Post

15 · The Genitive Expresses Possession

Die Arbeit	**des Studenten**
Das Auto	**meines Bruders**
Das Licht	**der Sonne**

The genitive case corresponds to the English possessive, or to the objective case preceded by *of*, which denotes possession in English.

A. *Restate the following sentences, supplying the correct forms of the missing endings:*

1. die Stärke d— Bären; der Mut d— Löwen; die List d— Fuchses
2. der Regent d— Landes; der Bürgermeister d— Stadt; die Pflicht d— Bürgers
3. die Bewohner d— Dörfer; die Bürger d— Städte; die Eigentümer d— Häuser
4. der Schein ein— brennenden Lampe; die Tage ein— langen Winters; die Spitze ein— hohen Berges
5. Das Ende dies— schönen Geschichte; der Tod dies— alten Mannes; das Werk jen— deutschen Dichters
6. die Bewohner dies— kleinen Land—; die Arbeit jen— fleißigen Student—; das Betragen jen— sonderbaren Mensch—

B. *Form the genitive:*

EXAMPLE: Das Buch gehört dem Lehrer; das ist das Buch **des Lehrers.**
Mein Vater hat einen Bruder; das ist der Bruder **meines Vaters.**

1. Das Auto gehört meinem Onkel.
2. Meine Mutter hat Geschwister.
3. Die Bürger des Landes haben Rechte.
4. Unsere Schwester hat Freundinnen.
5. Dieses Handwerkszeug gehört meinem Vater.
6. Dieses Geld gehört meiner Mutter.

C. *Restate the following sentences in German:*

1. Here is my brother's house. Tomorrow is my sister's birthday. This is my father's study.
2. The streets of this city are wide and clean.
3. The king of the country had died.
4. The master of the house was not at home.
5. He wanted half (*die Hälfte*) of the money.
6. We heard the voices of the people in the next room.
7. My mother's parents are living in the country.

16 · The Genitive After Certain Prepositions

	PREPOSITION	GENITIVE
Die Schule liegt	**diesseits**	des Marktplatzes.
Der Lehrer wohnt	**außerhalb**	der Stadt.
Ich besuche euch	**während**	meiner Ferien.
Er arbeitet viel	**trotz**	seines Alters.

The genitive case is used as the object of certain prepositions, the most common of which are: **außerhalb,** *outside of;* **innerhalb,** *inside of, within;* **oberhalb,** *above;* **unterhalb,** *below;* **diesseits,** *on this side of;* **jenseits,** *on the other side of;* **anstatt** or **statt,** *instead of;* **trotz,** *in spite of;* **während,** *during;* **wegen,** *because of, on account of.*

A. *Restate the following sentences, supplying the correct forms of the missing endings:*

1. Während d_ Ferien suche ich Arbeit in der Stadt.
2. Während d_ Winter_ gehe ich zur Schule.
3. Während d_ Tag_ bin ich immer in der Schule.
4. Samstags und sonntags bin ich viel außerhalb d_ Haus_.
5. Am Samstag, während d_ Vormittag_ helfe ich Mutter im Hause, während d_ Nachmittag_ bin ich frei.
6. Trotz ihr_ Alter– arbeitet Mutter noch viel im Hause.
7. Trotz sein_ großen Fleiß_ und trotz sein_ vielen Arbeit hat er das Examen nicht bestanden.
8. Karl wohnt jetzt diesseits d_ Park_, aber jenseits d_ Brücke.
9. Das Haus steht innerhalb ein_ Garten_.
10. Wegen d_ großen Entfernung, wegen d_ vielen Arbeit und wegen d_ Krankheit seiner Mutter konnte er uns noch nicht besuchen.

B. *Restate the following sentences in German:*

1. Do you live on this side or on the other side of the city?
2. I am living on the other side of the river, outside the city.
3. Within a week we will be on the other side of the ocean.
4. On account of his sickness he has to live in the South.
5. During the winter we will go to the theater often.
6. Are you going to school in spite of the rain?
7. Because (*wegen*) of the snow we cannot go to school.
8. Within an hour I will have finished my homework.
9. Father is always working during the evenings.
10. On account of the bad weather he is not coming.

17 · The Genitive Used Adverbially

Ich traf ihn	**eines Tages**	zufällig auf der Straße.
Ich ging	**eines Abends**	im Park spazieren.
Ich mache	**abends**	meine Schularbeiten.
Er war	**glücklicherweise**	nicht schwer verletzt.
Er ist	**jedenfalls**	schon abgereist.

a. The genitive case is used adverbially to express indefinite time and the time of usual or customary action: **eines Tages,** one (some) day; **morgens,** in the morning, mornings; **nachts,** at night; **sonntags,** on Sunday; **vormittags,** during the forenoon; **mittags,** at noon, etc.

b. The genitive of certain nouns, either alone or with an adjective, is also used to form adverbial expressions.

A. *Restate the following phrases and sentences in German:*

1. one day; one afternoon; one Sunday; in the evening; in the afternoon
2. late at night; early in the morning; nights; from early morning till late at night
3. In the morning my father goes to work, and I go to school.
4. School is out at four o'clock in the afternoon.
5. Evenings it is quiet in the streets of our city.
6. During the afternoon I like to play football.
7. One day he came to our house and spoke with my father.
8. Some day he will be a famous artist.
9. Do you sleep well at night?
10. The representatives assemble (*sich*) at noon.

B. *Restate the following sentences in English:*

1. Ich ging geradeswegs vom Theater nach Hause.
2. Allen Ernstes riet er mir, das Studium aufzugeben.
3. Er hörte die Nachricht und verließ schnellen Schrittes den Hörsaal.
4. Keinesfalls darfst du heute abend ausgehen.
5. Karl ist möglicherweise schon abgereist.

geradeswegs, *straightway*   allen Ernstes, *in all seriousness*
keinesfalls, *by no means*   möglicherweise, *possibly*
     schnellen Schrittes, *with swift steps (hastily)*

THE NOUN

18 · Declension of Proper Names and Titles

N.	Ulrich	Ute	Schiller	Goethe
G.	Ulrichs	Utes	Schillers	Goethes
D.	Ulrich	Ute	Schiller	Goethe
A.	Ulrich	Ute	Schiller	Goethe
N.	Gustaf Adolf	Maria Theresia	Alexander von Humboldt	
G.	Gustaf Adolfs	Maria Theresias	Alexander von Humboldts	

a. 1) Proper names of persons, when not preceded by a pronoun or article, form the genitive by adding the ending **-s**. 2) Combined names are treated as one word. 3) In the dative and accusative proper names remain unchanged.

A. *Give the genitive of the following proper names:*

1. Schiller_ Dramen.   Goethe_ Gedichte.   Heine_ „Harzreise".
2. Ulrich_ Arbeiten.   Kant_ Werke.   Ute_ Bruder.
3. Gustav Adolf_ Armee.   Maria Theresia_ Länder.   Alexander_ Reisen.

N.	Luise	Friederike	Marie	Luise Henriette
G.	Luises	Friederikes	Maries	Luise Henriettes

b. Feminine proper names ending in **-e**, formerly took in the genitive the ending **-ens**, but in present day writing they take just **-s**.

B. *Restate the following sentences with the genitive endings:*

1. Auf dem Tische fanden wir (Luise) Briefe.
2. (Friederike) Kinder starben alle in jungen Jahren.
3. (Marie) Eltern waren mir wohl bekannt.
4. (Luise Henriette) Freundinnen waren immer willkommene Gäste in unserm Hause.

N.		Franz	Max	Voß	Herkules
	FORMERLY:	Franz**ens**	Max**ens**	Voss**ens**	Herkuless**ens**
G.	NOW:	{Franz'	Max'	Voß'	Herkules'
		{des Franz	des Max	des Voß	des Herkules
		von Franz	von Max	von Voß	von Herkules

c. Masculine proper names ending in **-s, -ß, -sch, -z, -x** formerly took in genitive the ending **-ens.** Present day usage, however, marks the genitive either by the help of an apostrophe, or of the article, or, if possible, uses the preposition **von** instead of the genitive.

C. *Restate the following sentences using two or three forms of genitive:*

EXAMPLE: Der Bruder (Max) ist älter als ich.
Der Bruder **des Max** *or* **Max' Bruder** ist älter als ich.

1. Der Tod (Herkules) ist in der Literatur oft beschrieben worden.
2. Die Arbeit (Franz) ist besser als deine Arbeit.
3. Das Leben von (Voß) ist interessant zu lesen.

N.	der Heinrich	der arme Heinrich	dieser Karl	unsere Marie
G.	des Heinrich	des armen Heinrich	dieses Karl	unserer Marie
D.	dem Heinrich	dem armen Heinrich	diesem Karl	unserer Marie
A.	den Heinrich	den armen Heinrich	diesen Karl	unsere Marie

d. When preceded by an article or an adjective, proper names of persons remain uninflected throughout the singular.

D. *Restate the following sentences using the correct case of the proper name:*

1. Welchen Friedrich meinst du? Meinst du (Friedrich der Zweite)?
2. Der Vater (dieser Friedrich) war Wilhelm der Erste.
3. „Der arme Heinrich" ist eine Dichtung von (der Hartmann von Aue).
4. Fritz brachte (die Marie) ein Geschenk, hatte aber keins für Luise.

N.	Kaiser Karl der Große	Königin Elisabeth	Professor Dr. Roth
G.	Kaiser Karls des Großen	Königin Elisabeths	Professor Dr. Roths
N.	General von Waldersee	Mutter Heiser	Fräulein Schmidt
G.	General von Waldersees	Mutter Heisers	Fräulein Schmidts

e. Titles, expressions of relations, as **Frau, Fräulein, Onkel,** etc., may precede a proper name without article or pronoun. In this case, the proper name is inflected, but the appositive noun remains uninflected.

E. *Restate the following sentences supplying the missing genitive endings:*

1. Königin Elisabeth von England: Königin Elisabeth_ Schloß in London.
2. General Graf Terzky: General Graf Terzky_ Verrat.
3. Dr. Otto von Braun: Dr. Otto von Braun_ Studien.
4. Frau Mathilde Schlesinger aus Böhmen: Frau Mathilde Schlesinger_ Heimat in Böhmen.

N.	der alte Nestor	der reiche Krösus	der mächtige Karl
G.	des alten Nestor	des reichen Krösus	des mächtigen Karl
N.	der heilige Petrus	meine liebe Marie	mein lieber Heinrich
G.	des heiligen Petrus	meiner lieben Marie	meines lieben Heinrich

f. When preceded by an adjective, proper names must also be preceded by the article or by a pronoun. BUT: **der allmächtige Gott - des allmächtigen Gottes.**

F. *Restate the following sentences using the genitives:*

1. Die Griechen folgten dem Rat (der alte Nestor).
2. Der Reichtum und die Macht (der reiche Krösus) wurden viel beneidet.
3. Das Reich (der mächtige Karl) reichte von Deutschland bis nach Spanien.
4. Der Geburtstag (unsere liebe Marie) ist im Dezember.

THE ADJECTIVE

1 · Limiting Adjectives*

I. DER-WORDS

	Dieser	Schüler ist fleißig.
Ich habe die Arbeit	**dieses**	Schülers.
Ich gebe	**diesem**	Schüler das Buch.
Ich frage	**diesen**	Schüler.

The **der**-words** are declined like the definite article and agree in gender, number, and case with the nouns they modify.

A. *Decline in singular and plural the following nouns preceded by a* **Der-word:**

1. dieser Baum	diese Stadt	dieses Jahr
2. jener Satz	jene Geschichte	jenes Lied
3. welcher Arzt	welche Arbeit	welches Kind
4. mancher Soldat	manche Stunde	manches Jahr

B. *Restate the following phrases, supplying the missing endings:*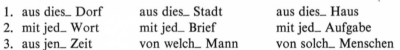

1. aus dies_ Dorf	aus dies_ Stadt	aus dies_ Haus
2. mit jed_ Wort	mit jed_ Brief	mit jed_ Aufgabe
3. aus jen_ Zeit	von welch_ Mann	von solch_ Menschen

C. *Restate the following sentences, supplying the missing endings:*

1. Setzen Sie sich auf dies_ Stuhl. Er sitzt auf dies_ Stuhl.
2. Hängen Sie das Bild an dies_ Wand. Das Bild hängt an dies_ Wand.
3. Gehen Sie in jen_ Haus. Er wohnt in jen_ Haus.
4. Ich habe manch_ Land und manch_ Stadt gesehen.
5. Ich glaube dies_ Mann, danke jen_ Frau, helfe jed_ Kind.

D. *Restate the following phrases and sentences in German:*

1. every father; every mother; every girl
2. which color; which dress; which man?
3. these years; these girls; these days
4. He came every afternoon, every week.

---

* *Limiting adjectives*, because they "limit" the following noun, and agree with it in gender, number and case, but do not "describe" it.
** **Der,** *the;* **dieser,** *this;* **jener,** *that;* **jeder,** *each, every;* **mancher,** *many a,* (plural *many*); **solcher,** *such, such a;* **welcher,** *which? what?*

THE ADJECTIVE

II. EIN-WORDS

	Kein	Mensch kann das verstehen.
Das Leben	**keines**	Menschen ist hier sicher.
Er spricht mit	**keinem**	Menschen.
Wir trafen	**keinen**	Menschen auf der Straße.

The **ein**-words* are declined like the indefinite article and agree in gender, number, and case with the nouns they modify.

A. *Decline in singular and plural the following nouns preceded by an* **Ein-word:**

1. kein Freund   keine Zeit   kein Lied
2. mein Vater   meine Mutter   mein Kind
3. dein Weg   seine Tochter   sein Recht
4. unser Geld   euer Spiel   ihr Geheimnis

B. *Restate the following phrases, supplying the missing endings:*

1. aus mein_ Garten;   aus sein_ Tasche;   aus ihr_ Glase
2. bei unser_ Nachbar;   bei ihr_ Freundin;   bei ihr_ Eltern
3. mit mein_ Erlaubnis;   mit dein_ Hilfe;   mit groß_ Plänen

C. *Restate the following sentences, supplying the missing endings:*

1. Trotz sein_ Fleißes und trotz sein_ vielen Arbeit fiel er im Examen durch.
2. Wir ziehen in euer_ Stadt, wohnen in euer_ Stadt; wohnen in euer_ Straße.
3. Er ist ein eigenartiger Mensch, er hilft kein_ Menschen, kein_ Nachbar, kein_ Kinde und spricht mit kein_ Leuten der Stadt.
4. Diese Geschichte gefällt unser_ Lehrer; unser_ Lehrerin, aber nicht mein_ Freunde Karl und sein_ Schwester Marie.

D. *Restate the following sentences in German:*

1. A hill outside our city.
2. He is sitting by (*an*) my side.
3. He is sitting down next to (*neben*) his friend.
4. He is going without my permission.
5. She is helping her mother.

---

* **Ein,** *a, an;* **kein,** *no, not any;* **mein,** *my;* **dein,** *your;* **sein,** *his;* **ihr,** *her;* **sein,** *its;* **unser,** *our;* **euer,** *your;* **ihr,** *their;* **Ihr,** *your.*

THE ADJECTIVE

2 · Descriptive Adjectives Used as Predicate and as Adverbs

Die Luft ist	**frisch** und **rein.**	
Der Winter war	**lang** und **kalt.**	
Der Sommer wird	**heiß** und **trocken.**	
Regentropfen,	**groß** und **schwer,**	fallen zur Erde.
Blumen,	**rot** und **weiß,**	blühen im Garten.
Wolken,	**dunkel** und **schwer,**	stehen am Himmel
Es regnete	**stark** und **viel.**	
Der Wind wehte	**kalt**	durch die Bäume.
Es ist oft	**außerordentlich**	heiß hier.

Descriptive adjectives never take an ending: 1) when used as predicate adjectives with such verbs as **sein** and **werden;** 2) when they follow the noun which they describe; 3) when they are used as adverbs.

A. *Read the following sentences and observe the use of adjectives as predicate or as adverbs and restate in English:*

1. Im Sommer sind die Tage länger als im Winter und die Nächte kürzer.
2. Das Wetter ist angenehm, die Tage sind warm, aber die Nächte sind kühl.
3. Die Aussicht von diesem Berge war herrlich und reichte weit über das Tal.
4. In der letzten Nacht hat es viel und stark geregnet.
5. Vater kam aufgeregt und ärgerlich ins Zimmer.
6. Er gab den Armen gern und reichlich von allem, was er hatte.
7. Kinder, klein und groß, gingen die Straße hinab zur Schule.
8. Mädchen, jung und schlank, standen vor den Türen.
9. Schnee, weich und schwer, bedeckte die Erde.

B. *Restate the following sentences in German:*

1. The man was young and strong.
2. The road became steep and monotonous.
3. The streets in this old city are narrow and dark.
4. They lived happily together.
5. He had an army, large and powerful.
6. People, young and old, poor and rich, gathered in front of the city hall.
7. A man, tall and slender, spoke to the people.

3 · Weak Declension of Attributives*

I. PRECEDED BY EIN-WORDS

	SINGULAR	*das*
kein armer Mann	keine arme Frau	kein armes Kind
keines armen Mannes	keiner armen Frau	keines armen Kindes
keinem armen Mann	keiner armen Frau	keinem armen Kind
keinen armen Mann	keine arme Frau	kein armes Kind

	PLURAL	
keine armen Männer	keine armen Frauen	keine armen Kinder
keiner armen Männer	keiner armen Frauen	keiner armen Kinder
keinen armen Männern	keinen armen Frauen	keinen armen Kindern
keine armen Männer	keine armen Frauen	keine armen Kinder

Preceded by an **ein**-word,** attributive adjectives take the weak ending **-en**, except in five forms in the singular: the nominative masculine and neuter and the accusative neuter take the strong endings **-er, -es, -es**, respectively; the nominative and accusative feminine take the ending **-e**.

A. *Decline the following phrases, in both singular and plural:*

1. kein lang_ Weg; dein bös_ Feind; sein gut_ Recht
2. unser_ klein_ Stadt; ihr groß_ Reich; kein glücklich_ Mensch

B. *In the following sentences supply the missing endings:*

1. Er ist ein Schüler unser_ deutsch_ Klasse.
2. Was haben Sie in Ihr_ recht_ Hand?
3. Das war kein groß_ Verlust für mich.
4. Mit ein_ fest_, unbeugsam_ Willen verfolgte Karl sein Ziel.***
5. Ich wartete an ein_ windig_ und belebt_ Straßenecke.

C. *Restate the following sentences in German:*

1. A good book is a good friend.
2. He bought a new and expensive auto.
3. These houses belong to our hard-working, thrifty, rich neighbor.
4. I wrote a letter and thanked my dear, old, and kind mother.

---

* A descriptive adjective preceding a noun is called an *attributive adjective.*
** See: ein-words, page 83.
*** When there are several attributive adjectives, preceding a noun, they all have the same case endings.

SINGULAR		
der arme Mann	diese arme Frau	jenes arme Kind
des armen Mannes	dieser armen Frau	jenes armen Kindes
dem armen Mann	dieser armen Frau	jenem armen Kind
den armen Mann	diese arme Frau	jenes arme Kind
PLURAL		
die armen Männer	diese armen Frauen	jene armen Kinder
der armen Männer	dieser armen Frauen	jener armen Kinder
den armen Männern	diesen armen Frauen	jenen armen Kindern
die armen Männer	diese armen Frauen	jene armen Kinder

Preceded by a **der**-word,* attributive adjectives take the weak ending **-en**, except in five forms in the singular: the nominative masculine, feminine, and neuter, and the accusative feminine and neuter, in which they take **-e**.

A. *Decline the following phrases in German, in both singular and plural:*

1. das letzte Jahr;   dieser kalte Winter;   jene langweilige Vorlesung
2. welcher gute Arzt?   solche böse Tat;   manches schöne Lied

B. *Supply the missing endings:*

1. Haben Sie dies_ Geschichte gelesen?
2. Kennen sie jen_ fremd_ Mädchen?
3. Wo ist die Mutter dies_ klein_ Kinder?
4. Was haben Sie jen_ arm_ Leuten gegeben?
5. Jed_ fleißig_ Arbeiter hat ein Recht auf sein_ Lohn.
6. Manch_ jung_ tapfer_ Soldat ist im letzt_ Kriege gefallen.
7. Von welch_ berühmt_ Manne sprechen Sie?
8. Er wohnt in jen_ klein_, alt_ Haus.

C. *Restate the following sentences in German:*

1. I saw that old beautiful church.
2. I visited those foreign countries and saw many interesting places.
3. I like these German books and those German newspapers.
4. What is the name of this quaint old place?
5. This man is a famous writer, and he can tell you many an interesting story.
6. Such beautiful and colorful flowers do not grow in our country.

---

* See: **der**-words, page 82.

4 · Strong Declension of Attributives

SINGULAR		
heißer Kaffee	süße Milch	kaltes Wasser
heißen Kaffees	süßer Milch	kalten Wassers
heißem Kaffee	süßer Milch	kaltem Wasser
heißen Kaffee	süße Milch	kaltes Wasser

PLURAL		
N. gute Männer	gute Frauen	gute Kinder
G. guter Männer	guter Frauen	guter Kinder
D. guten Männern	guten Frauen	guten Kindern
A. gute Männer	gute Frauen	gute Kinder

If no limiting adjective (**der**-word or **ein**-word) precedes the attributive adjective, the attributive adjective assumes the function and the full declensional endings of the **der**-words, except in the genitive singular, masculine and neuter, where the -en ending has supplanted the original -es. This is called the *strong declension* of the adjective.*

A. *Decline the following phrases in singular and plural:*
  1. kurzer Tag; lange Nacht; ernstes Gesicht
  2. guter, treuer Freund; schwere, schwarze Wolke; langes, blondes Haar

B. *Supply the missing endings:*
  1. Es ist ein Kind reich_ Leute, von gut_ Familie, aus gut_ Haus.
  2. Ein Mädchen mit blond_ Haar, klar_ blau_ Augen und von schlank_ Gestalt öffnete die Tür.
  3. Gut_ Essen, alt_ Wein, schwarz_ Kaffee und für die Kinder süß_ Milch, reif_ Obst, weiß_ Brot und frisch_ Butter stellte der Wirt auf den Tisch.

C. *Restate the following sentences in German:*
  1. Young and old, poor and rich people went to church.
  2. Write your lesson with black ink on (*auf*) white paper.
  3. Our city has wide streets, beautiful buildings and large gardens with high old trees.
  4. He spoke to me in (*mit*) [a] loud, deep voice.

D. *Say it in English:*
  1. „Die wahre Bildung besteht nicht in totem Wissen und leerem Gedächtniskram, sondern in lebendiger Entwicklung des Gemüts und der Urteilskraft des Verstandes." (Haeckel)

* See *Synopsis of Grammar*, p. 163.

THE ADJECTIVE

5 · Comparison of Adjectives

POSITIVE	COMPARATIVE	SUPERLATIVE	
klein*	kleiner*	am kleinsten*	der kleinste
heiß	heißer	am heißesten	der heißeste
alt	älter	am ältesten	der älteste
jung	jünger	am jüngsten	der jüngste
edel	edeler	am edelsten	der edelste
dunkel	dunkler	am dunkelsten	der dunkelste
gut	besser	am besten	der beste

a. The comparative of an adjective is formed by adding -er, the superlative by adding -st or -est to the positive.

b. A number of adjectives take umlaut in the comparative and superlative:

arm, ärmer, ärmst   from, frömmer, frömmst
kurz, kürzer, kürzest   klug, klüger, klügst
groß, größer, größest   lang, länger, längst

c. Adjectives ending in -e, -el, -en, -er drop the -e- before the comparative ending:

weise, weiser   selten, seltner   tapfer, tapfrer
finster, finstrer   teuer, teurer   sicher, sichrer

d. A number of very common adjectives and adverbs have irregular or defective forms in the comparative and superlative:

viel, mehr, am meisten, der meiste   hoch, höher, am höchsten
gut, besser, am besten, der beste   nah, näher, am nächsten
gern (*adverb*) lieber, am liebsten   bald (*adverb*) eher, am ehesten

A. *Restate the following sentences using the superlative form of the adjective:*

1. Der Sturm begann um Mitternacht und war am (heftig) gegen Morgen.
2. Er war der (gewandt) und (klar) Redner, den ich je gehört habe.
3. Am (interessant) war der Bericht über seine Reise durch das (unbekannt) Afrika.

B. *Restate the following sentences using the correct comparative form of the adjective:*

1. Gestern machten wir einen länger_ Spaziergang durch die weiter_ Umgebung der Stadt.
2. Er gehört zu den besser_ Schülern in meiner Klasse.
3. Der Rhein ist bekannt_, schön_ und berühmt_ als alle anderen Flüsse in Deutschland.

---

* Note that these are forms of adjectives used as predicate or as adverbs.

THE NUMERAL

1 · Cardinal Numbers

0 null,	1 eins,	2 zwei,	3 drei,	7 sieben,
10 zehn,	11 elf,	12 zwölf,	13 dreizehn,	17 siebzehn,
20 zwanzig,	21 einundzwanzig,	32 zweiunddreißig,		
58 achtundfünfzig,	100 hundert,	101 hundertundeins,		
102 hundertundzwei,	200 zweihundert,	205 zweihundertundfünf,		
1000 tausend,	1001 tausendundeins,			

1961 neunzehnhundert einundsechzig *oder*
tausendneunhundert einundsechzig

a. Cardinals, with the exception of **eins,** are usually uninflected.

A. *Restate in English:*

1. Die Woche hat sieben Tage.
2. Zwölf Monate sind ein Jahr.
3. Ich habe drei Dollar, Ernst hat sieben.
4. Dieser Mann ist über hundert Jahre alt.

b. Eins is used only when it stands by itself or is the final element of a compound.

B. *Restate in English:*

1. Es ist halb eins.
2. Es war im Jahre hundertundeins.
3. Ich kaufte ein Buch, er kaufte auch eins.

c. As a numeral adjective, **eins** is declined like the indefinite article but receives a heavy accent.

C. *Restate in English:*

1. Ich sehe nur einen Mann, nicht zwei.
2. Das Konzert dauerte nur eine Stunde, nicht ein und eine halbe Stunde.
3. Ich weiß es bestimmt, er hatte nur einen Sohn, nicht drei.

d. *Once, twice, three times,* etc. are formed in German by adding **-mal** to the cardinal.

D. *Restate in English:*

1. Wir leben nur einmal in der Welt.
2. Schreiben Sie das Wort zweimal an die Wandtafel.
3. Er ist fünfmal nicht zur Klasse gekommen.

e. *Half past* is expressed in German by **halb** with the following hour.

E. *Restate in English:*

1. Meine Schule beginnt um *halb neun.*
2. Meine Schule ist um *halb vier* aus.
3. Wir essen Mittag um *halb eins.*

f. *A quarter past* may be expressed by **ein Viertel** with the following hour or by **ein Viertel nach** with the preceding hour.

F. *Restate in English:*

1. Es ist Viertel zwei.
2. Es ist Viertel nach eins.
3. Es ist Viertel sieben.
4. Es ist Viertel nach sechs.

g. *A quarter of* is expressed either by **Viertel vor** or by **drei Viertel** with the following hour.

G. *Restate in English:*

1. Es ist Viertel vor sieben.
2. Es ist drei Viertel sieben.
3. Es ist Viertel vor neun.
4. Es ist drei Viertel neun.

h. Distinguish between **Uhr** (o'clock) and **Stunde** (hour): **Uhr** means definite time, **Stunde** means duration of time.

H. *Restate in English:*

1. Wieviel Uhr ist es? Es ist zehn Uhr.
2. Ich komme um fünf Uhr. Ich bleibe bis acht Uhr.
3. Ich habe jeden Tag vier Stunden Unterricht.
4. Ich habe nur eine halbe Stunde Zeit.

2 · Ordinal Numbers

(der, die, das)	(*the*)	(der, die, das)	(*the*)
1. erste	1*st*	11. elfte	11*th*
2. zweite	2*nd*	12. zwölfte	12*th*
3. dritte	3*rd*	13. dreizehnte	13*th*
4. vierte	4*th*	19. neunzehnte	19*th*
5. fünfte	5*th*	20. zwanzigste	20*th*
7. siebente	7*th*	21. einundzwanzigste	21*st*
8. achte	8*th*	100. hundertste	100*th*
10. zehnte	10*th*	101. hunderterste	101*st*

a. Ordinals are adjectives formed from the corresponding cardinals by adding the suffix -te to the cardinal up to nineteen, and the suffix -ste from twenty upwards. Note the irregular forms of: **der erste, der dritte, der achte.**

A. *Restate the following phrases with their ordinals:*

1. Der 11. Oktober;   der 21. November;   der 1. Januar
2. Der 5. März;   der 30. Januar;   der 17. September

	SINGULAR	PLURAL
N.	mein erstes Buch	meine ersten Bücher
G.	meines ersten Buches	meiner ersten Bücher
D.	meinem ersten Buch	meinen ersten Büchern
A.	mein erstes Buch	meine ersten Bücher

b. Ordinals are declined like attributive adjectives.

B. *Decline in singular and plural:*

1. das erste Lied;   der fünfte Tag;   dieser zweite Sonntag
2. dein viertes Jahr;   mein zweiter Wunsch;   kein vierter Mann.

> Der vierte (*or* 4.) Juli ist in diesem Jahr ein Sonntag.
> Der einundzwanzigste (*or* 21.) Mai ist mein Geburtstag.
> Berlin, den 30. September 1967.

c. A period after a numeral indicates that the numeral is to be read as an ordinal. In letters the date is always in the accusative case.

C. *Restate the following sentences in German:*

1. School begins again on the 24th of September.
2. America was discovered on the 12th of October 1492.
3. Christmas is on the 25th of December.
4. Denver, July 30, 1967.

D. *Restate in English:*

„Der Mensch hat dreierlei Wege klug zu handeln: erstens durch Nachdenken, das ist der edelste; zweitens durch Nachahmen, das ist der leichteste; drittens durch Erfahrung, das ist der bitterste."

(Confuzius)

THE ADVERB

1 · The Function of Adverbs

Vater ist **eben** (*just now*) fortgegangen.
Ich habe den Mann **selten** (*seldom*) gesehen.
Er ist **keineswegs** (*by no means*) dumm oder faul.
Es ist ein **wirklich** (*really*) gutes Buch.
Ich habe diese Geschichte **besonders** (*especially*) gern.
Er ist ein **nie** (*never*) ganz zufriedener Mensch.

Whenever a closer definition of the activity indicated by a verb or a special emphasis of the meaning of an adjective or adverb appears necessary or desirable, an adverb is used. Adverbs are used to modify verbs, adjectives, and other adverbs.

Restate the following sentences in English (*see the list of adverbs below*)*:*

1. Er schreibt nicht oft, er schreibt selten, oder nie.
2. Warum arbeiten Sie so viel? Sie arbeiten immer. Arbeiten Sie nicht zu viel.
3. Lernst du nichts in der Schule? Warum lernst du so wenig? Du spielst immer und träumst meistens in der Schule. Ich lerne etwas, wenn auch nicht viel.
4. Kommt er heute, oder kommt er später? Ist er bald hier, und bleibt er lange?
5. Er ist wahrscheinlich krank, denn ganz gesund war er nie, und er ist nicht immer vorsichtig. -
6. Ich wohne gern in der Stadt; ich wohne lieber auf dem Lande; ich wohne am liebsten an der See.
7. Dies ist ein höchst interessantes Buch, und es kostet mindestens fünf Dollar.

oft, *often*	meistens, *mostly*	ganz, *quite, entirely*
selten, *seldom*	etwas, *something*	nie, *never*
viel, *much*	heute, *today*	gern, *like to*
immer, *always*	später, *later*	lieber, *prefer to*
zu viel, *too much*	bald, *soon*	am liebsten, *the most*
nichts, *nothing*	lange, *long* (*time*)	höchst, *highly*
wenig, *little*	wahrscheinlich, *probably*	mindestens, *at least*

2 · Adverbs of Time

Ich gehe **jetzt** zu einer Vorlesung in Geschichte.
Mein Freund Karl ist **wochenlang** krank gewesen.
Jetzt ist er gesund und macht **täglich** seine Arbeiten.
Er ist **eben** zur Vorlesung gekommen.

Adverbs of time indicate when the verbal act is taking place; they answer the German questions: **Wann? Wie lange? Seit wann? Wie oft?**

The most common adverbs of time are:

a) ADVERBS EXPRESSING INDEFINITE TIME:

einst, *once upon a time*	**manchmal,** *at times*
einmal, *once*	**meistens,** *most of the time*
früher, *formerly*	**wenig,** *little*
später, *later*	**oft,** *often, frequently*
bald, *soon*	**zuweilen,** *at times*
gleich, *immediately*	**kürzlich,** *recently*
nachher, *afterwards*	**zuerst,** *at first*
endlich, *finally*	**stundenlang,** *for hours*

b) ADVERBS EXPRESSING DEFINITE TIME:

anfangs, *at first*	**täglich,** *daily*
eben, *just now*	**heute,** *today*
jetzt, *now, at present*	**gestern,** *yesterday*
nun, *now*	**abends,** *in the evening*
nie, *never*	**nachts,** *at night*
sofort, *at once*	**sonntags,** *on Sundays*
immer, *always*	**heutzutage,** *nowadays*

A. *Restate the following sentences in English:*

1. Ich habe täglich eine Stunde Deutsch und wöchentlich zwei Stunden Musik.
2. Unser Professor ist immer gut vorbereitet, eben kommt er ins Klassenzimmer.
3. Abends mache ich meine Schularbeiten, sonntags arbeite ich nicht.
4. Anfangs waren unsere Aufgaben leicht, jetzt werden sie schwerer.

B. *Restate the following sentences in German:*

1. Are you never at home?
2. I just came home.
3. He is quite often unprepared.
4. He is recently out of work.
5. He is always ready to help.

3 · Adverbs of Place

Was machst du **da**? Wie geht es dir **dort**?
Ist das Leben **dort** angenehmer als **hier**?
Wohnst du **drinnen** in der Stadt,
   oder wohnst du **draußen**?
Arbeitest du **dort**, oder wohnst du nur **da**?

Adverbs of place indicate where the verbal act is taking place. They answer the German questions: **Wo? Woher? Wohin?**

The most common adverbs of place are:

hier, *here;*
   hierhin, *to this place;*
   von hier, *from this place*
dort, *there;*
   dorthin, *there;*
   nach dort, *to that place*
da, *there;*
   dahin, *to that place;*
   von da, *from there*
außen, *outside;*
   draußen, *outside;*
   nach draußen, *outside*
innen, *inside;*
   drinnen, *inside, from within;*
   von drinnen, *from the inside*

oben, *above;*
   nach oben, *up, up to;*
   von oben, *from above*
unten, *below;*
   nach unten, *downwards;*
   drunten, *down there, below*
vorn, *in front, at the beginning;*
   nach vorn, *forward;*
   von vorn, *from the front*
rechts, *to the right, on the right;*
   von rechts, *from the right;*
   nach rechts, *to the right*
-wärts, *-ward;*
   abwärts, *downward;*
   vorwärts, *forward, in front*

A. *Restate the following sentences in English:*

1. Ich wohne hier, aber ich komme von dort.
2. Regnet es dort bei euch in Florida?
3. Hier schneit es seit drei Tagen.
5. Warum stehst du draußen, geh' doch nach drinnen.
6. Unten im Hause ist es wärmer als oben.
7. Der Motor ist hinten im Auto, nicht vorn.
8. An der Straßenkreuzung müssen Sie nach rechts und nicht nach links abbiegen.
9. Unser Weg führte abwärts in ein Tal hinein.
10. Von oben ist die Aussicht schöner als hier von unten.

4 · Adverbs of Manner, Measure, and Degree

> Hat er diese Arbeit **wirklich** selber gemacht?
> **Wahrscheinlich** hat ihm jemand dabei geholfen.
> Er ist im Kriege **dreimal** verwundet worden.
> Dr. Frank hat **vergebens** versucht ihm zu helfen.

Adverbs of manner describe in what manner or to what degree the verbal act is taking place. They answer the German questions: **Wie? In welcher Weise?**

The most common adverbs of manner are:

wirklich, *really, truly*	**vielleicht,** *perhaps*
wahrscheinlich, *probably*	**unversehens,** *unexpectedly*
plötzlich, *suddenly*	**vergebens,** *in vain*
gewöhnlich, *usually*	**wohl,** *possibly, perhaps*
augenblicklich, *immediately*	**ganz,** *quite, entirely*
noch, *still, yet*	**fast,** *almost, nearly*
gern *gladly, like to*	**kaum,** *hardly, barely*
meistens, *mostly*	**genug,** *enough*
ziemlich, *rather, fairly*	**etwas,** *somewhat, a little*
doch, *yet, please, of course*	**viel,** *much, often*

A. *Restate the following sentences in English:*

1. Augenblicklich habe ich nicht das Geld zu einer Reise.
2. Wenn ich reise, so reise ich gewöhnlich im Herbst.
3. Hoffen wir! Vielleicht haben wir morgen besseres Wetter.
4. Du irrst dich, Karl ist wirklich kein dummer Mensch.
5. Ich habe gestern vergebens auf dich gewartet.
6. Du hast wohl nicht die Zeit zum Ausgehen gehabt.
7. Wartet ein wenig, ich gehe gern mit.
8. Im Monat Mai ist es hier ziemlich kalt und meistens regnet es auch.
9. Kommen Sie doch herein, es gibt hier viel zu sehen.
10. Unversehens war die Mutter ins Zimmer gekommen, und alles Streiten unter den Kindern hörte plötzlich auf.
11. Das neue Schulgesetz ist in der Zeitung dreimal angezeigt worden.
12. Ich habe dir das nicht dreimal, ich habe es dir schon zehnmal gesagt: Rauchen ist hier verboten.

5 · Adjectives Used as Adverbs

> Der Schauspieler hat seine Rolle **gut** gespielt.
> Die Schauspielerin war für ihre Rolle **schön** gekleidet.
> Ihr Gesang klang in dem großen Saal **höchst** angenehm.
> Wir sind **länger** geblieben, als wir wollten.
> Die Schauspielerin sang und spielte **am besten.**

a. In most cases, when adjectives are used as adverbs, they are used without change of form: **gut, schön.** They can be used also in their comparative and superlative form: **höchst, länger, am besten.** *

b. "Regular" adverbs: **kaum, genug, ganz,** etc., are, in general, not subject to comparison, but there are a few exceptions. **

A. *Restate the following sentences in English:*

1. Der Soldat kam schwer verwundet aus der Schlacht zurück.
2. Die Sonne schien heiß auf die ausgedörrte Erde herab.
3. Die Sterne standen kalt und klar am nächtlichen Himmel.
4. Das Meer lag still und ruhig vor uns.
5. Er sprach leise und eindringlich auf uns ein.
6. Seit Jahren schon arbeitet er fleißig und sorgfältig an diesem Projekt.
7. Er ist niemals unhöflich oder ungeduldig gewesen.
8. Er trat unversehens und unerwartet ins Zimmer.
9. Er ist mehrfach, aber immer vergebens gewarnt worden.
10. Karl arbeitet in diesem Semester fleißiger und regelmäßiger als ich.
11. Der Wind wurde stärker und stärker, das Wetter schlechter und schlechter und der Weg steiler und steiler und wir kamen müde oben auf dem Berge an.
12. Oben auf dem Berge war es am kältesten, der Wind am stärksten und der Regen am heftigsten.
13. Wir waren aufs höchste überrascht, dort oben Leute zu finden, wurden aber von ihnen aufs freundlichste begrüßt.

---

* See p. 88.
** **oft - öfter; häufig - häufiger; selten - seltener. Ander** and **besonder** add **-s**: *Ex.* Hier ist vieles **anders** geworden. Er war nicht **besonders** bekannt in der Stadt.

THE PRONOUN

1 · List of Pronouns

NOM.	ich	du	er	sie	es	
GEN.	meiner	deiner	seiner	ihrer	seiner	
DAT.	mir	dir	ihm	ihr	ihm	→ sich
ACC.	mich	dich	ihn	sie	es	

PLURAL   REFLEXIVE

NOM.	wir	ihr	sie	Sie	
GEN.	unser	euer	ihrer	Ihrer	
DAT.	uns	euch	ihnen	Ihnen	→ sich
ACC.	uns	euch	sie	Sie	

II. RELATIVE PRONOUNS

SINGULAR   PLURAL

	Masc.	*Fem.*	*Neut.*	*Masc.*	*Fem.*	*Neut.*	M.F.N.	M.F.N.
N.	der	die	das	welcher	welche	welches	die	welche
G.	dessen	deren	dessen	(*lacking*)	(*lacking*)	(*lacking*)	deren	(*lacking*)
D.	dem	der	dem	welchem	welcher	welchem	denen	welchen
A.	den	die	das	welchen	welche	welches	die	welche

III. INDEFINITE RELATIVE PRONOUNS

SINGULAR

NOM.	wer	was
GEN.	wessen	——
DAT.	wem	——
ACC.	wen	was

IV. INDEFINITE PRONOUNS

man, *one, they, people*
einer, irgendeiner, *one, somebody*
jemand, *somebody, someone*
niemand, *nobody, no one*
keiner, *nobody, no one*

jeder, *everyone*
alle, *everybody, all*
viel, viele, *much, many*
einige, *several*
wenig, wenige, *little, a few*

THE PRONOUN

2 · Personal Pronouns

SINGULAR					
ich, *I*	du	Sie	er	sie	es**
meiner, *of me**	deiner	Ihrer	seiner	ihrer	seiner
mir, *to me, me*	dir	Ihnen	ihm	ihr	ihm
mich, *me*	dich	Sie	ihn	sie	es
PLURAL					
wir, *we*	ihr	Sie		sie	
unser, *of us*	euer	Ihrer		ihrer	
uns, *to us, us*	euch	Ihnen		ihnen	
uns, *us*	euch	Sie		sie	

A. *Supply the proper form of the personal pronoun in each of the following phrases.*

> EXAMPLE: Er fragt nach (ich);   er wohnt bei (wir).
> Er fragt nach **mir**;   er wohnt bei **uns**.

1. Er spricht von (du); er geht ohne (du); er geht mit (sie, *sing.*).
2. Er sitzt bei (ich); er steht vor (ich); er setzt sich neben (ich).
3. Du gehst mit (er); du gehst mit (sie, *sing.*); er kommt von (wir).
4. Er geht zu (ihr, *pl.*); sie arbeitet für (er); er arbeitet für (sie).
5. Er grüßt (ich); er ruft (er); er ruft (wir); er grüßt (du).

B. Mir *oder* **mich; dir** *oder* **dich**? *in the following phrases add the missing personal pronouns and give the English meaning of the phrase.*

> EXAMPLE: Fürchte —— nicht;   Wasche —— die Hände
> Fürchte dich nicht;   Wasche dir die Hände.
> *Don't be afraid;*   *Wash your hands.*

---

* The genitive of a personal pronoun is very rarely used in German, since it cannot depend upon a noun. It is used with a few adjectives and verbs and also partitively. These forms are rare: **Ich bin seiner müde,** *I am tired of him.* **Herr, gedenke meiner!** *Lord, be mindful of me!* **Es waren ihrer drei,** *There were three of them.*

** Note the use of **es** in the following phrases:

Wer ist's?	*Who is it?*	Ich bin's.	*It's I.*
Wir sind's.	*It's we.*	Bist du's?	*Is it you?*
Sie sind's.	*It is they.*	Seid Ihr's?	*Is it you?*
Was gibt's?	*What's the matter?*		
	Hier gibt's zu tun. *Here is work to be done.*		
	Wie geht's? *How are you?*		

1. Kämme _____ das Haar; reinige _____ die Schuhe; nimm _____ in acht.
2. Pflücke _____ ein paar Blumen, nimm _____ ein Stück Kuchen.
3. Diese Arbeit gelingt _____ nicht; es freut _____, dich zu sehen.
4. Diese Sache geht _____ nichts an; gib _____ etwas zu essen.
5. Bringe _____ etwas aus der Stadt mit; zeige _____ deine neue Uhr.
6. Lassen Sie _____ heute Fußball spielen; bitte, leihen Sie _____ ihr Buch.
7. Bitte, holen Sie _____ heute abend ab; seien Sie _____ nicht böse.
8. Laß _____ das Geld nicht stehlen; erkundige _____ nach dem rechten Weg.

C. *Restate the following sentences, replacing each noun by a proper pronoun.*

EXAMPLE: Die Kinder lachten über den Schulmeister.
Sie   lachten über   **ihn.**

1. Der Lehrer sprach zu den Kindern.
2. Die Kinder hörten dem Lehrer zu.
3. Die Kinder fürchteten sich vor dem Lehrer.
4. Die Lehrer helfen den Kindern.
5. Karl hat an Elisabeth geschrieben.
6. Elisabeth wohnt bei ihrer Mutter.
7. Die Mutter ärgerte sich über Elisabeth.
8. Vater hat das Auto nicht gekauft.
9. Karl hat seine Füllfeder verloren.
10. Marie hat ihre Schularbeit vergessen.
11. Die Leute glaubten dem Manne nicht.

D. *Restate the following sentences in German.*

EXAMPLE: *Who is it? Is it you, Karl? Is it you, Mr. Braun?*
Wer ist **es**? Bist du **es**, Karl? Sind Sie **es**, Herr Braun?

1. Do you love me? Do you love him? Do you love her?
2. I don't see you; do you see me? don't you see us?
3. Didn't you show him your new watch?
4. He and I have been traveling much together.
5. Neither I nor you had studied the lesson.

3 · Pronominal Compounds with <u>Da-</u> and <u>Dar-</u>

Hier ist ein Ball;	spiele	mit dem Ball.
		mit ihm.
		damit.
Der Vorschlag ist gut;	ich stimme	für den Vorschlag.
		für ihn.
		dafür.
Viele schöne Bücher,	aber kein deutsches	unter den Büchern.
		darunter.
Ein guter Gedanke,	wie denken Sie	über den Vorschlag?
		darüber?

After prepositions, personal pronouns with reference to an inanimate object (and also when the reference is more general) may be replaced by the adverb **da** (**dar** before a vowel) plus a preposition. In the same manner the adverb **hier** plus preposition may be used. Adverb and preposition are written together as one word: **daran, darauf, daraus, dabei, dadurch, dafür, dagegen, damit, danach** or **darnach, darüber, darunter, davon, dazu, dazwischen; hiermit, hierauf.**

A. *Observe the use of the pronominal compounds in German and restate the following sentences in English:*

1. Es ist ein guter Vorschlag, warum sind Sie dagegen? (*against it*)
2. Das ist alles, was ich darüber weiß. (*about it*)
3. Das ist meine Meinung, und dabei bleibe ich. (*stick to it*)
4. Komm pünktlich um sechs Uhr, ich zähle darauf. (*count on it*)
5. Hast du deine Schularbeiten gemacht? Ich bin gerade dabei. (*at it*)
6. Es war eine große Versammlung, es waren auch viele Frauen darunter. (*among them*)
7. Wer baut das Haus, und wer gibt das Geld dazu? (*for it*)
8. Schicken Sie mir sofort das Buch, ich bitte drum.* (*for it*)
9. Es war ein langer Brief, aber es stand kein Name drunter. (*under it*)
10. Er hielt sein Wort und arbeitete fleißig, und ich war sehr froh drüber. (*about it*)
11. Der Wein ist gut, geben Sie mir noch ein Glas davon. (*of it*)
12. Meine geplante Reise? Ich fürchte, es wird nichts draus. (*nothing will come of it*)

---

* The compound **dar-** often (especially in colloquial language) drops the vowel -a-: **dran, draus, drauf, drüber, drunter, drum.**

B. *Restate in English:*

1. „Ich habe mich durch eigene Erfahrung daran gewöhnt, alle Misere dieses Lebens als unbedeutend und vorübergehend zu betrachten und dabei fest an die Zukunft zu glauben."

(Gottfried Keller)

2. „Ein kleines Lied, wie geht's nur an,
   Daß man so lieb es haben kann?
   Was liegt darin? Erzähle!
   Es liegt darin ein wenig Klang,
   Ein wenig Wohllaut und Gesang,
   Und eine ganze Seele."

(Ebner Eschnenbach)

4 · The Relative Pronouns <u>Der</u> and <u>Welcher</u>

	Masc.	*Fem.*	*Neut.*	*Masc.*	*Fem.*	*Neut.*	M.F.N.	M.F.N.
N.	der	die	das	welcher	welche	welches	die	welche
G.	dessen	deren	dessen	(*lacking*)	(*lacking*)	(*lacking*)	deren	(*lacking*)
D.	dem	der	dem	welchem	welcher	welchem	denen	welchen
A.	den	die	das	welchen	welche	welches	die	welche

a. 1) The relative pronoun **der, die, das** is declined like the definite article, except in the genitive singular (**dessen, deren, dessen**) and in the genitive plural (**deren**) and dative plural (**denen**). 2) The relative pronoun **welcher, welche, welches** is declined like the **der**-words, except for the genitive case which **welcher** lacks and which is supplied by the genitive of **der**. 3) **Der, die, das** and **welcher, welche, welches** can be used interchangeably.

RELATIVE		SUBORDINATE CLAUSE
Der Bauer,	**der**	diese Geschichte erzählte, ist mir bekannt.
Der Bauer,	**dem**	das Pferd gehörte, war im Wirtshaus.
Das Kind,	**dessen**	Vater gestorben ist, braucht Geld.
Ich fand das Haus,	**das**	ich suchte.
Die Leute,	**welche**	in diesem Lande wohnen, sind arm.

b. 1) The relative pronouns **der** and **welcher,** used to introduce subordinate clauses,* refer always to an expressed antecedent, either persons or things. 2) They agree with their antecedents in gender and number; case is determined by their function in the sentence. 3) The relative pronoun cannot be omitted in German as in English.

A. *Restate the following sentences in German, supplying the relative pronouns which have been omitted:*

1. Der Student, _____ eben in die Klasse kommt, ist Herr Schmidt.
2. Die Studentin, _____ eben liest, heißt Fräulein Braun.
3. Der Mann, _____ das Geld gestohlen worden war, suchte den Dieb.

---

* See section on word order, p. 128.

4. Ich fand die Kinder, ____ ich suchte, im Garten spielen.
5. Die Leute, ____ ich diese Geschichte erzählte, glaubten mir nicht.
6. Mein Freund Karl, ____ ich diese Geschichte erzählte, glaubte mir nicht.
7. Die Kinder, ____ in dieser Gegend wohnen, sind meistens arme Kinder.
8. Die Bücher, ____ wir nicht mehr gebrauchen, bringen wir in die Bibliothek zurück.
9. Die Bücher, aus ____ wir gelernt haben, bringen wir in die Bibliothek zurück.
10. Das Buch, für ____ ich fünf Dollar bezahlt habe, habe ich verloren.
11. Die Ferien, auf ____ ich so lange gewartet habe, sind endlich gekommen.
12. Das Fest, auf ____ ich mich so gefreut habe, ist mir verdorben worden.
13. Der Wald, durch ____ wir Soldaten marschierten, schien unendlich groß zu sein.

B. *In the following sentences supply the relative pronoun and restate the sentences in English:*

1. „So selten kommt der Augenblick im Leben, ____ wahrhaft wichtig ist und groß.“

   (Schiller)

2. „Nur nach dem Baum, ____ Früchte trägt, wirft man mit Steinen.“

   (Arabisch)

3. „Wer über gewisse Dinge den Verstand verliert, ____ hat keinen zu verlieren.“

   (Lessing)

4. „Den Ruhm großer Männer soll man immer nach den Mitteln bemessen, mit ____ sie sich ihren Ruhm erworben haben.“

   (La Rochefoucauld)

5. „Wir lieben immer die Menschen, ____ uns bewundern; aber wir lieben nicht immer diejenigen, ____ wir bewundern.“

   (Grillparzer)

6. „Der Charakter ist ein Fels, an ____ gestrandete Schiffer landen, und anstürmende scheitern.“

   (Kant)

5 · The Relative Pronouns <u>Wer</u> and <u>Was</u>

RELATIVE   SUBORDINATE CLAUSE

Wer reich ist,	(der) ist nicht immer glücklich.
Wer nicht arbeitet,	(der) soll auch nicht essen.
Wer krank ist,	soll zum Arzt gehen.
Was er gekauft hat,	sagt er uns nicht.
Es ist alles wahr,	**was** er sagt.
Das ist das Beste,	**was** ich habe.

Wer and **Was**, meaning *whoever, whatever, he who, that which,* are used as generalizing or indefinite relatives.

A. *Restate the following sentences, supplying* **wer** *or* **was,** *as required:*

1. _____ essen will, soll auch arbeiten.
2. _____ lügt, der stiehlt auch.
3. _____ nicht studiert, verschwendet nur sein Geld.
4. _____ man ehrlich will, kann man gewöhnlich auch tun.
5. _____ drei wissen, wissen auch bald hundert.
6. _____ der Löwe nicht kann, das kann oft der Fuchs.
7. Ich wußte nicht, _____ ich zu dem Vorschlag sagen sollte.
8. Ich glaube nicht alles, _____ Sie mir sagen.
9. Nicht alles, _____ glänzt, ist Gold.
10. Nicht _____ wenig hat, sondern _____ sich viel wünscht, ist arm.
    (Seneca)
11. _____ immer zu Hause bleibt, bleibt im Witz zurück.
    (Shakespeare)
12. _____ nicht wert ist, mehr als einmal gelesen zu werden, verdient nicht, überhaupt gelesen zu werden.
    (C. J. Weber)
13. Ein Held ist, _____ sein Leben großen Dingen opfert; _____ es für ein Nichts hingibt, ist ein Narr.
    (Grillparzer)

B. *Restate the following sentences in German:*

1. He who knows this man will respect him.
2. He who wants to work should have the right to work.
3. Only he who has the money can buy this painting.
4. It was the best I could get for my money.

5. A single penny is all I have.
6. What a man wishes he readily believes.
7. "What I have written, I have written!"

C. *Say it in English:*

1. „Wer sich um Weisheit und Kenntnis bemüht, und nicht anwendet die Weisheit und Kenntnis, der ist wie ein Mann, der pflügt und zu säen vergißt."

(Herder)

2. „Was man in der Jugend wünscht (Zeit), hat man im Alter die Fülle."
(Goethe)

3. „Am Abend (*evening of life*) duftet alles, was man gepflanzt hat, am lieblichsten."

(Leisewitz)

4. „Wer nicht Musik hat in ihm selbst,
Wen nicht die Eintracht süßer Töne rührt,
Taugt zu Verrat, zu Ränken und zu Tücken.
Die Regung seines Sinns ist dumpf wie Nacht,
Sein Trachten düster wie der Erebus.
Trau keinem solchen."

(Shakespeare)

6 · Compounds with <u>Wo-</u> and <u>Wor-</u>

Es war das Auto	**für das**	er viel Geld bezahlt hatte.
	wofür	
Der Friede	**auf den**	wir warten, kommt nicht.
	worauf	

After prepositions which govern the dative or the accusative case, relative pronouns with reference to an inanimate object may be replaced by a pronominal compound consisting of the adverb **wo** or **wor** (before a vowel) and the desired preposition: **worauf, woran, wofür, wobei, woraus, wodurch, wovon, wozu,** etc.*

A. *Observe the use of the pronominal compounds in German and restate the following sentences in English:*

1. Ich erhielt eben Ihren Brief, woraus (aus dem) ich ersehe, daß Sie eine neue Stellung angenommen haben.
2. Das Material, woraus (aus dem) diese Kette gemacht ist, ist eine Mischung aus Silber und Nickel.
3. Das Glas, woraus (aus dem) ich eben getrunken hatte, zersprang plötzlich in meiner Hand.
4. Es war ein freudiges Wiedersehen und eine herzliche Begrüßung, wobei (bei der) uns die Tränen in die Augen kamen.
5. Das Gestein, worauf (auf das) wir unser Haus bauen, ist Felsgestein.
6. Es ist ein Mittel, womit (mit dem) man Ratten und Mäuse aus den Wohnhäusern vertreiben kann.
7. Das Ziel, wonach (nach dem) er strebte, hat er jetzt erreicht.
8. Alles, woran (an was) er denkt und was er plant, ist Geld und Reichtum.
9. Eine Anzahl von Büchern lag auf dem Tisch, worunter (unter denen) einige von großem Wert waren.
10. Es geschehen Dinge in der Welt, wogegen (gegen die) vieles zu sagen ist.

---

* Although pronominal compounds are very common in popular speech and widely used, there is in choice language, spoken or written, a decided preference for the inflected pronominal form.

THE CONJUNCTION

Conjunctions

I. CO-ORDINATING CONJUNCTIONS

II. SUBORDINATING CONJUNCTIONS

Ich vertraute ihm,	**aber**	er enttäuschte mich.
Ich verkaufte das Haus,	**denn**	ich brauchte das Geld.
Mein Vater	**und**	meine Mutter besuchten mich.
Ich hoffte	**und**	wartete auf bessere Zeiten.
Es war zehn Uhr,	**als**	ich nach Hause kam.
Er schreibt mir eben,	**daß**	er nicht kommen kann.
Ich weiß nicht,	**wo**	er augenblicklich ist.

a. Conjunctions are words used to connect sentences or the elements of a sentence. As in English, they are divided into co-ordinating and subordinating conjunctions.

The most common co-ordinating conjunctions are:

aber, *but*   **allein,** *but*   **sondern,** *but on the contrary*
und, *and*   **oder,** *or*   **denn,** *for*
                 entweder . . . oder, *either . . . or*
                 weder . . . noch, *neither . . . nor*
                 sowohl . . . als (auch), *both . . . and*

b. Co-ordinating conjunctions exert no influence upon the word order.

The most common subordinating conjunctions are:

als, *when, as*   **als ob,** *as if*   **bevor,** *before*
bis, *until*   **da,** *as, since* (casual)   **damit,** *in order that*
daß, *that, so that*   **ehe,** *before*   **indem,** *while*
nachdem, *after*   **ob,** *whether*   **obgleich,** *although*
seitdem, *since* (temporal)   **sobald,** *as soon as*   **während,** *while*
wann, *when* (in indirect   **weil,** *because, since*   **wenn,** *if, when,*
 questions)   **wo,** *where* (in indirect   *whenever*
wie, *how, as* (manner)   discourse)

c. In sentences introduced by subordinating conjunctions the finite verb stands at the end of the clause.*

---

* See section on word order, p. 117.

A. Connect the following pairs of sentences by using the indicated conjunctions:

1. Wir konnten nicht ausgehen. Das Wetter war zu schlecht. (weil, denn)
2. Karl konnte seine Studien nicht beenden. Er hatte nicht das Geld dazu. (denn, weil)
3. Ich verließ die Universität. Ich mußte das Geschäft meines Vaters übernehmen. (denn, weil)
4. Ich folgte dem Rat meines Vaters. Ich hatte den Rat nicht besonders gern. (obgleich, aber)
5. Ich habe gestern abend arbeiten müssen. Ich wäre lieber mit Marie in ein Konzert gegangen. (obgleich)
6. Ich kam heute etwas später nach Hause. Ich hatte noch einige Sachen im Geschäft zu tun. (da)
7. Ich weiß nicht, wer der Mann gewesen ist. Er wollte mir seinen Namen nicht sagen. (da, weil)
8. Wir verließen das Haus und gingen in den Garten. Wir durften in dem Hause nicht rauchen. (denn, da)
9. Er beantwortete meinen Brief nicht. Ich habe ihm in der letzten Woche zweimal geschrieben. (obgleich)
10. Professor Braun fragt in diesem Brief an. Hast du sein neuestes Buch gelesen? (ob)
11. Du mußt mir die Antwort auf diesen Brief zeigen. Du bringst den Brief zur Post. (ehe)
12. Man kann klüger sein als ein anderer. Man kann nicht klüger sein, als alle anderen. (aber)
13. Der Geizhals tut niemandem etwas Gutes. Er behandelt sich selbst am schlechtesten. (aber)
14. „Jeder Tag sollte so gestaltet werden. Er beende die Reihe der Tage und erfülle das Leben restlos." (als wenn)

(Seneca)

15. „Nichts kränkt den Menschen tiefer. Da, wo er Liebe und Wohlwollen erwarten darf, findet er nicht einmal die geringste Gerechtigkeit" (als wenn er)

(v. Hartmann)

B. Use in the following sentences the proper conjunction: aber, sondern, allein:*

1. Der Mann ist durchaus nicht alt, _____ im Gegenteil noch recht jung.
2. Das Wetter ist heute nicht schön, _____ wir können besseres Wetter erwarten.

---

* Of the three conjunctions aber, sondern, allein, aber occurs most frequently, and its position in the clause is very free; sondern must always stand first in the clause and may be used only when it introduces an affirmative statement which excludes or is to be substituted for a preceding negative one; allein must always stand first in the clause and is more literary and rather rare.

3. Er konnte weder schreiben noch lesen, ____ er war durchaus nicht dumm.
4. Er wollte mir das Buch nicht schenken, ____ er wollte es mir nur leihen.
5. Er ist nicht einer von den begabtesten meiner Schüler, ____ er ist nur ein sehr fleißiger Schüler.
6. Ich vertraute fest auf ihn, ____ er hat mich bitter enttäuscht.
7. Ich habe fleißig an dieser Aufgabe gearbeitet, ich konnte sie ____ nicht fertigbringen.
8. Ich wollte dich gestern besuchen, du bist ____ nicht zu Hause gewesen.
9. Er ist kein guter, ____ im Gegenteil ein sehr schlechter Geschäftsmann gewesen.
10. Karl blieb nicht auf der Universität, ____ nach ein paar Semestern gab er sein Studium auf.
11. Herr Schmidt hat in seinem Leben viele Sachen versucht und begonnen, ____ (*use:* allein) es ist ihm nirgends geglückt.
12. Er gewann zwar den Krieg, ____ (*use:* allein) ihm fehlte die Klugheit, einen dauernden Frieden zu schließen.

C. *Restate the following sentences in German:*

1. I sold the book after I had read it.
2. She wants to know whether you could call for her tomorrow.
3. I'll talk to him when he comes home tonight.
4. Show me your homework before you hand it in.
5. While I was looking for my book I found this letter.
6. Do you believe that he is telling the truth?
7. Do you think that you can do this work?
8. He made no mistakes in his test because he had prepared his lesson well.
9. I'll ask her if I see her.
10. I know that she is unhappy, although she does not show it.

WORD ORDER

1 · Independent Clauses:*
Normal Word Order, Simple Tenses

SUBJECT	FINITE VERB	MODIFIERS OF THE VERB
Der Lehrer	**spricht**	mit meinem Vater.
Der Student	**arbeitet**	im Laboratorium.
Der Schüler	**macht**	seine Schularbeit.
Mein Vater	**sandte**	mir das Geld.

In all independent sentences the finite verb** is the second element in the sentence (Normal Word Order).

A. *Complete the following sentences, using one of the given modifiers:*

1. Der Schüler lernt ＿＿
2. Der Student arbeitet ＿＿
3. Marie liest ＿＿
4. Der Vater geht ＿＿
5. Meine Eltern reisen ＿＿
6. Wir besuchen ＿＿
7. Das Buch lag ＿＿
8. Das Haus stand ＿＿
9. Ein kleiner Garten lag ＿＿
10. Die Kinder waren ＿＿
11. Meine Schwester wartete ＿＿
12. Wir gingen ＿＿

ein deutsches Gedicht	in der Bibliothek	eine deutsche Novelle
in sein Geschäft	nach Deutschland	unsere Großeltern
auf seinem Schreibtisch	am Marktplatz	hinter dem Haus
noch in der Schule	auf ihre Freundin	alle ins Theater

B. *Restate the following sentences in English:*

1. Zeit ist Geld.
2. Aller Anfang ist schwer.
3. Die Erde ist ein Planet.
4. Alle Menschen müssen sterben.
5. Sieben Tage sind eine Woche.
6. Hilf deinem Freund!
7. Verschwende nicht dein Geld!
8. Der Gesunde braucht keinen Arzt.
9. Es fällt kein Meister vom Himmel.

C. *Restate the following sentences in German:*

1. I am going home.
2. I am studying my lesson.
3. She writes her homework.
4. He is closing his book.
5. He needs my help.
6. My friend is coming tomorrow.
7. You didn't answer my question.
8. I don't believe the man.

---

* That is: principal clauses, or independent sentences.
** By finite verb is meant that part of the predicate which takes the personal endings: in simple tenses the verb, in compound tenses the auxiliary.

2 · Independent Clauses:
Normal Word Order, Compound Tenses

SUBJECT	FINITE VERB	MODIFIERS	PARTICIPLE OR INFINITIVE
Er	hat	seinen Lehrer	gegrüßt.
Er	ist	zur Schule	gegangen.
Du	wirst	zur Universität	kommen.
Er	wird	morgen den Brief	geschrieben haben.

In sentences employing compound tenses of the verb the finite verb (auxiliary) is the second element, the participle and the infinitive stand last, the participle preceding the infinitive in cases in which both are used (Normal Word Order).

A. *Restate the following sentences in the present perfect tense:*

1. Ich lerne dieses Gedicht.
2. Ich gehe heute nicht zur Vorlesung.
3. Ich bleibe bis vier Uhr im Lesezimmer.
4. Ich bringe alle meine Bücher zur Bibliothek.
5. Karl begleitet mich auf meiner Reise nach Deutschland.

B. *Restate the following sentences in the future tense:*

1. Ich schreibe einen Brief an meine Freundin.
2. Ich frage meinen Professor um Rat.
3. Wir haben morgen das Schlußexamen für dieses Semester.
4. Nach dem Schlußexamen beginnen unsere Ferien.
5. Ich fahre dann zu meinen Eltern nach Hause.

C. *Restate the following sentences in the future perfect tense:*

1. Ich sehe meinen Advokaten morgen um zehn Uhr.
2. Er lernte das lange Gedicht gestern abend.
3. Die Kinder spielten den ganzen Vormittag Fußball.
4. Karl ist mit seinen Freunden ins Gebirge gefahren.
5. Er hat die Gewalt über sein Auto verloren.

D. *Restate the following sentences in German in the present perfect tense:*

1. My father bought this house.
2. He wrote a letter to (*an*) his parents.
3. He speaks too (*zu*) rapidly.
4. I met the old gentleman in our city park.
5. Mary and Karl went home after the lecture.

3 · Independent Clauses: Inverted Word Order

EMPHASIZED PART	FINITE VERB	SUBJECT	
Heute morgen	machte	ich	einen Spaziergang.
Für meine Schwester	kaufte	er	gestern das Geschenk.
Meine Schularbeit	hatte	ich	vergessen.
Im Theater	habe	ich	ihn gestern gesehen.

a. When for emphasis any sentence unit other than the subject introduces the independent sentence, the finite verb stands as second element, the subject as third (Inverted Word Order).

b. In an independent sentence in German the subject either precedes the finite verb (Normal Word Order), or follows the finite verb immediately (Inverted Word Order).

A. *Restate the following sentences, beginning each sentence with the expression of time:*

1. Wir fuhren an einem Sonntag von New York nach Boston.
2. Mein Bruder ist den ganzen Tag über in der Schule gewesen.
3. Er ist eben nach Hause gekommen.
4. Er lebt jetzt hier bei uns in der Stadt.
5. Mein Vater ist heute plötzlich nach Hamburg abgereist.
6. Im Hamburger Flughafen landet das Flugzeug nach sechs Stunden.

B. *Restate the following sentences, starting each sentence with the adverb or adverbial phrase:*

1. Er konnte endlos von seinen Reisen und Erlebnissen erzählen.
2. Ich habe noch niemals eine Antwort von ihm bekommen.
3. Sie ist gleich nach Hause gegangen, als ihre Mutter sie rief.
4. Ich will mit ihr morgen abend ins Theater gehen.
5. Er ist noch kurz vorher als lieber Gast bei uns gewesen.

C. *Restate the following sentences in German, starting with the italicized words:*

1. She went home *immediately* after school.
2. The sun sets *in summer* at half past eight.
3. I will leave New York *at half past nine*.
4. He has given me *some money*.
5. Next Sunday we shall play *football* again.

4 · Independent Clauses:
Word Order of Questions

	VERB	SUBJECT	
	Gehen	Sie	heute ins Theater?
	Sind	Sie	gestern im Theater gewesen?
Wann	gehen	Sie	heute abend ins Theater?
Warum	gehen	Sie	heute abend nicht ins Theater?
Mit wem	gehen	Sie	heute abend ins Theater?

In questions the finite verb stands first. If, however, the question is introduced by an interrogative (pronoun, adverb, or phrase) this interrogative is the first unit and is directly followed by the finite verb.

A. *On each of the following statements formulate questions: 1) without an interrogative; 2) with an interrogative:*

1. Vater arbeitete den ganzen Tag. (warum)
2. Die Kinder spielten den ganzen Nachmittag Fußball. (wo)
3. Karl ging heute morgen nicht zur Vorlesung. (warum)
4. Er hat mit seinem Auto einen Unfall gehabt. (wann)
5. Er ist von New York nach Deutschland abgefahren. (wann)
6. Dr. Frank hält einen Vortrag über die Geschichte Süd-Afrikas. (wo)
7. Professor Schmidt hält eine Vorlesung über die Geschichte der medizinischen Wissenschaft. (wann)
8. Professor Schmidt lehrte zwanzig Jahre lang an dieser Universität (wie lange)
9. Er studierte vier Jahre lang auf dieser Universität. (wie viele Jahre lang)

B. *Restate the following questions in German:*

1. When will you read this German book?
2. Where are my books?
3. When will you go to Germany?
4. Where did you buy this beautiful painting?
5. What did he say to you?
6. What did you have for (*zum*) breakfast?
7. Why did you not answer my letter?
8. To whom do these books belong?
9. With whom will you travel this summer?
10. For whom are you buying this present?
11. Did you visit the city of Heidelberg?

5 · Independent Clauses:
Compound Verbs with Separable Prefixes

SUBJECT	VERB	MODIFIERS	PREFIX
Ein alter Mann	ging	langsam die Straße	hinab.
Er	kehrte	von einem Spaziergang	zurück.
Der Mann	stand	vor einem Hause	still.
Er	stieg	langsam eine Treppe	hinauf.

In an independent clause, separable prefixes of compound verbs stand at the end of the clause.*

A. *Restate the following sentences, using: 1) the present tense; 2) the past tense of the indicated compound verb (make certain that the verb and prefix are in correct position):*

1. Der Mann (ausruhen) von seinem Spaziergang.
2. Die Straße (hineinführen) direkt in die Stadt.
3. Er (fortsetzen) seinen Spaziergang durch den Park.
4. Für diesen kleinen Dienst er (annehmen) keine Belohnung.
5. Mit dieser Arbeit ich (aufhören) jetzt.
6. Mutter (einkaufen) einige Sachen in der Stadt.
7. Sie (mitbringen) einige kleine Geschenke für die Kinder.
8. In Erwartung der Geschenke die Kinder (entgegenlaufen) ihrer Mutter.
9. Ich (aufhalten) mich hier in der Stadt eine Woche lang.
10. Vater (vorlesen) uns die Geschichte von dem Untergang der „Bremen."
11. Karl und ich (vorbereiten) uns auf das nächste Examen in der Physik und in Geschichte.
12. Karl (zurückbringen) mir einige Bücher, die er von mir vor langer Zeit geliehen hatte.

B. *Restate the following sentences in German:*

1. The sun rises at six o'clock (*use: aufgehen*).
2. The sun sets at half past six (*use: untergehen*).
3. Father gets úp at half past six (*use: aufstehen*).
4. Our guests went away at ten o'clock (*use: weggehen*).
5. When did you return home? (*use: zurückkommen*).

---

* See section on compound verbs, page 19.

6 · Independent Clauses:
Place of Indirect and Direct Object

	INDIRECT OBJECT	DIRECT OBJECT
Er zeigte	**dem Freunde**	das Bild.
Er sandte	**seiner Mutter**	die Blumen.
Er gab	**mir**	den Schlüssel.

	DIRECT OBJECT	INDIRECT OBJECT
Er zeigte	es	**dem Freunde.**
Er sandte	sie	**seiner Mutter.**
Er gab	ihn	**mir.**

If the direct object is expressed by a noun, the indirect precedes; but if the direct object is a personal pronoun, this order is reversed.

A. *Restate the following sentences: 1) with the direct object expressed by the proper pronoun; 2) with the indirect object expressed by the proper pronoun:*

1. Ich gebe dem Schüler das Buch.
2. Ich zeige dem Lehrer die Schularbeit.
3. Ich habe meinem Freunde das Geld geliehen.
4. Er schickte seiner Freundin diese Blumen.
5. Mutter gab der armen Frau etwas Geld.
6. Mutter erzählte den Kindern eine kleine Geschichte.
7. Vater hat den Kindern diese Geschenke gesandt.

B. *Restate the following sentences with both the direct and indirect object expressed by pronouns:*

1. Ich gebe dem Schüler das Buch.
2. Ich zeige dem Lehrer die Schularbeit.
3. Er schickt seiner Mutter Blumen.
4. Mutter gab der armen Frau etwas Geld.

C. *Restate the following sentences in German:*

1. I have given him some money.
2. He bought a watch for his son.
3. He showed it to me.
4. I showed it to her.
5. I sold it (*die Uhr*) to him.

7 · Independent Clauses: Position of <u>Nicht</u>

Ich habe das Buch	**nicht.**
Er antwortete mir	**nicht.**
Er hatte seine Schularbeit	**nicht.**

a. Nicht, with the simple tenses, stands at the end of the clause.

IN THE COMPOUND TENSES

Ich werde das Buch	**nicht**	lesen.
Ich habe das Buch	**nicht**	gelesen.
Er hat mir	**nicht**	geantwortet.

b. Nicht, with compound tenses, precedes the infinitive and the participle.

PRECEDING A SEPARABLE PREFIX

Er machte die Tür	**nicht**	zu.
Ich gehe heute abend	**nicht**	aus.
Der Student kam	**nicht**	zurück.

c. Nicht precedes a separable prefix.

PRECEDING A PREDICATE ADJECTIVE, ETC.

Mein Bruder ist	**nicht**	krank.
Mein Bruder ist	**nicht**	hier.
Mein Bruder ist	**nicht**	Arzt.
Mein Bruder geht	**nicht**	in diese Schule.

d. Nicht precedes a predicate adjective or adverb, a predicate noun, and a predicate phrase.

WORD ORDER

> **Nicht** der Vater, sondern die Mutter hat geschrieben.
> **Nicht** er ist reich, sondern sein Bruder.
> Er ist **nicht** in die Kirche, sondern in die Schule gegangen.
> Es ist meine Schwester gewesen und **nicht** mein Bruder.

e. When it modifies a particular word or phrase, **nicht** stands immediately before this word or phrase.

A. *Restate the following sentences as negative sentences employing* **nicht**:

1. Er glaubte mir.
2. Ich fragte ihn.
3. Er hat seine Schularbeit.
4. Ich vergesse das.
5. Verlieren Sie das Geld.
6. Lesen Sie diese dumme Geschichte.
7. Sonntags gehen wir zur Schule.
8. Mutter ist heute zu Hause.
9. In diesem Sommer reisen wir nach Mexiko.
10. Werfen Sie die Zeitung auf den Fußboden.
11. Rauchen ist hier in diesem Hause verboten.
12. Unser Professor hat heute seine Vorlesung gehalten.
13. Ich habe mir das teure Auto gekauft.
14. Er gab seine geplante Reise nach Italien auf.
15. Vor zehn Uhr abends hört er mit seiner Arbeit auf.
16. Vor acht Uhr morgens kommt das Flugzeug in Berlin an.
17. Er bereitete sich auf das Schlußexamen vor.
18. Mein Bruder ist Arzt und auch Professor.
19. Er hat seine Arbeit gut gemacht und hat das Examen auch bestanden.
20. Wir haben unsern Lehrer gesehen und auch gesprochen.

B. *Restate the following sentences in German:*

1. My friend Ernst was not at home.
2. He was not in school either.
3. My father is not sick.
4. I did not get your letter.
5. He could not find his German book.
6. He can do it, but he doesn't want to.
7. Don't believe him.
8. He is not stupid, he is only lazy.
9. I could not understand what he said.
10. Not he, but his sister has written.

WORD ORDER **125**

8 · Independent Clauses:
Double Infinitive with Modal Auxiliaries*

	INFINITIVE	INFINITIVE
Ich habe den ganzen Tag	arbeiten	**müssen.**
Ich habe diese Aufgabe nicht	beenden	**können.**
Er hat unser Haus nicht	kaufen	**wollen.**
Sie wird heute nicht	ausgehen	**dürfen.**
Sie wird nicht haben**	ausgehen	**dürfen.**

In the commonly called 'double infinitive' construction—where an infinitive is dependent upon a modal auxiliary in a perfect or future tense—the modal auxiliary stands last in the sentence, always in the form of the infinitive.

A. *Restate the following sentences: 1) in the present perfect tense; 2) in the future tense:*

1. Das Kind durfte nicht auf der Straße spielen.
2. Wir dürfen nicht länger bleiben, wir müssen bald nach Hause gehen.
3. Ich mag diese Arbeit nicht machen, aber ich muß sie machen.
4. Zuerst wollte der Mann nicht antworten, aber auf die Frage des Richters mußte er antworten.
5. Ich konnte seine schlechte Handschrift nicht lesen, ich mußte ihm seine Arbeit zurückgeben.
6. Er wollte nicht Deutsch sprechen, er konnte nicht gut Deutsch sprechen.
7. Ich darf heute abend ausgehen, aber ich will heute nicht ausgehen.
8. Das Kind will nicht zur Schule gehen, aber es muß zur Schule gehen.

B. *Restate the following sentences in German, using the present perfect tense:*

1. I was not allowed to stay.
2. He wanted to buy the horse.
3. He was not able to carry the load.
4. We had to go home.
5. What did you want to say?
6. I can't find my watch.
7. I didn't like to see the man.

---

* See section on double infinitive constructions, page 32.
** Note the position of **haben** with the future perfect tense.

9 · Independent Clauses:
Attributive Participle or Adjective

ARTICLE		PARTICIPLE WITH MODIFIERS*	NOUN
Er war	ein	in Berlin sehr **bekannter** und **beliebter**	Künstler.
Es ist	ein	seit langen Jahren viel **gelesenes**	Buch.
Alkohol ist	ein	zu diesem Zwecke höchst **brauchbares**	Mittel.

An attributive participle or adjective precedes its noun and is itself preceded by its own modifiers.

The participle construction given above may be changed into relative clauses as follows:

Er war ein Künstler, der in Berlin sehr bekannt und beliebt war.
He was an artist well known and popular in Berlin.
Es ist ein Buch, das seit langen Jahren viel gelesen wird.
It is a book widely read for many years.
Alkohol ist ein Mittel, das zu diesem Zwecke höchst brauchbar ist.
Alcohol is a remedy highly useful for this purpose.

A. *Restate the following sentences in German, changing the participle construction to a relative clause, and translate into English:*

1. Er wohnte in einem alten, ursprünglich nicht zu Wohnzwecken bestimmten Gebäude.
2. Der seinerzeit von allen Mitbürgern der Stadt hochgeachtete und geehrte Pfarrer Schmidt starb gestern unbeachtet und von allen vergessen.
3. Der im kommenden Herbst in der allgemeinen Wahl die meisten Stimmen erhaltende Kandidat ist für die nächsten zwei Jahre Bürgermeister unserer Stadt.
4. Das aus Mitteln der Stadtkasse und freiwilligen Beiträgen der Bürger gebaute neue Theater unserer Stadt wird am kommenden Sonntag eingeweiht werden.
5. Die auf diese Weise aus einem Teil Wasserstoff einem Teil Stickstoff und drei Teilen Sauerstoff durch Mischung gewonnene Säure heißt Salpetersäure.

---

* This 'participle construction' is now condemned by German stylists, but it is still used by journalists, business men, and especially by writers of technical and scientific works and articles.

10 · Subordinate Clauses:
Introduced by Relative Pronouns

PRONOUN		FINITE VERB	
Der Mann, der	vor dem Hause	**steht,**	ist mein Vater.
Der Mann, dessen	Haus wir	**kaufen,**	ist unser Nachbar.
Der Mann, dem	wir das Geld	**leihen,**	ist ehrlich.
Der Mann, den	ich eben	**grüßte,**	ist mein Lehrer.
Die Frau, die	uns besucht	**hat,**	ist Frau Schmidt.
Die Frau, deren	Mann gestorben	**ist,**	ist unsere Nachbarin.
Die Frau, der	wir eben begegnet	**sind,**	ist eine Ärztin.
Die Frau, die	wir sprechen	**wollen,**	ist meine Lehrerin.

In subordinate clauses introduced by relative pronouns the finite verb stands at the end of the clause.

A. *Restate the following sentences, changing the clauses in parentheses to subordinate clauses, introduced by a relative pronoun:*

1. Der Mann, (er kommt eben ins Zimmer), ist Professor Mayer.
2. Die Studentin, (sie sitzt dort am Fenster), ist Fräulein Schulz.
3. Das Bild, (es hängt dort an der Wand), zeigt eine Straße in Japan.
4. Der Mann, (ich war der Gast dieses Mannes), ist ein alter Freund meines Vaters.
5. Der Arzt, (wir haben sofort den Arzt gerufen), konnte nicht mehr helfen.
6. Der Mann, (du hast ihn gestern in unserm Hause gesehen), ist ein Künstler.
7. Die Häuser, (sie werden dort am Fluß gebaut), sind alle schon verkauft.
8. Die Leute, (Vater hat ihnen diese Häuser verkauft), wollen im nächsten Monat einziehen.

B. *Say it in English:*

1. „Leicht ist es, ein kleines Feuer auszutreten, das, erst geduldet, Flüsse nicht mehr löschen können.“

   (Shakespeare)

2. „Ein Held ist, wer sein Leben großen Dingen opfert. Wer es für ein Nichts hingibt, ist ein Narr.“

   (Grillparzer)

3. „Jede Zeit ist ein Rätsel, das nicht die Zeit selber, sondern immer erst die Zukunft löst.“

   (v. Ihering)

11 · Subordinate Clauses:
Introduced by Subordinating Conjunctions

PRINCIPAL CLAUSE	CONJUNCTION	SUBORDINATE CLAUSE	VERB
Es war zehn Uhr,	als	ich nach Hause	**kam.**
Ich weiß nicht,	wo	er augenblicklich	**ist.**
Ich sage es ihm,	wenn	er nach Hause	**kommt.**
Es ist doch klar,	daß	ich das nicht tun	**kann.**
Es ist nicht wahr,	daß	ich morgen schon	**abreise.**
Wir werden gehen,	sobald	du fertig sein	**wirst.**
Ich habe gearbeitet,	während	er draußen gespielt	**hat.**
Vater fragte mich,	wo	ich gewesen	**sei.**

In subordinate clauses introduced by subordinating conjunctions the finite verb stands at the end of the clause. (See Conjunctions, p. 113.)

A. *Connect the following pairs of German sentences by using the indicated subordinating conjunctions:*

1. Ich werde hier warten. Du kommst zurück. (bis)
2. Man läutet die Glocke. Man tritt in ein Haus. (ehe)
3. Wir suchten Schutz unter einem Baum. Es fing zu regnen an. (als)
4. Er antwortete mir nicht. Ich fragte ihn zweimal. (obgleich)
5. Ich schreibe Ihnen. Ich habe Zeit. (sobald)
6. Er schreibt mir eben. Er kann nicht kommen. (daß)
7. Ich habe ihm Geld geschickt. Er kann nach Hause kommen. (damit)
8. Was wirst du tun? Du bist mit deinen Studien fertig. (nachdem)
9. Ich tue es. Ich habe Ihre Erlaubnis dazu. (sobald)
10. Er kann nicht mehr gut sehen. Er ist schon über achtzig Jahre alt. (weil)

B. *Restate the following sentences in German:*

1. He wants to know whether you have read yesterday's paper. (*ob*)
2. I will ask him when I see him. (*wenn*)
3. I saw her when I went to school yesterday. (*als*)
4. He is not happy although he has everything in the world. (*obgleich*)
5. He closed the book and put it away after he had read the first page. (*nachdem*)
6. I had to wait until he was ready to see me. (*bis*)
7. I am not going along because I am busy and have to work. (*weil*)
8. He made many mistakes although he had prepared his lesson quite well. (*obgleich*)

12 · Subordinate Clauses:
Preceding Principal Clause

SUBORDINATE CLAUSE	VERB	PRINCIPAL CLAUSE
Wenn ich Geld habe,	**gehe**	ich ins Theater.
Während wir in der Schule waren,	**brach**	das Feuer aus.
Bevor ich zu Bett gehe,	**schließe**	ich Fenster und Türen.
Als ich ins Haus trat,	**schlug**	die Uhr elf.

In complex sentences the subordinate clause often precedes the main or independent clause. In this case, the finite verb of the main clause stands first in its clause. (The subordinate clause may be regarded here as the first unit of the sentence, equivalent to an adverb or adverbial phrase.)*

A. *In the following sentences reverse the order of the independent and subordinate clauses:*

1. Mein Freund Werner kam ins Zimmer, während ich mich zum Ausgehen fertig machte.
2. Er fragte mich, wo ich hingehen wolle.
3. Ich antwortete ihm, daß ich heute nicht mehr arbeiten wolle.
4. Ich habe ihn nicht mehr gesehen, seit er die Universität verlassen hat.
5. Ich bleibe in diesem Hause wohnen, solange ich nicht etwas Besseres finde.
6. Er sah mich erstaunt und fragend an, als ich in sein Zimmer trat.
7. Ich werde euch wieder besuchen, wenn ich wieder nach Chicago komme.

B. *Restate the following sentences in German:*

1. When father is home, he reads and plays with us.
2. As long as he has been here, he has been sick.
3. Whenever he visits us, he always brings me a gift.
4. After he had left us, we missed him very much.
5. Where he is living, I don't know.
6. While looking for a book, I found this old letter.
7. If I close the door, it will be too warm in this room.
8. While we were visiting your parents, your brother arrived.
9. That he can do that work, do you believe that?
10. That he is telling the truth, can he prove it?

---

* See chapter on inverted word order, page 120.

SYNOPSIS OF GRAMMAR

1 · Principal Parts of Strong Verbs

INFINITIVE	MEANING	PAST INDICATIVE	PAST PARTICIPLE
beginnen	*to begin*	begann	begonnen
beißen	*to bite*	biß	gebissen
besinnen (sich)	*to remember*	besann	besonnen
betrügen	*to deceive*	betrog	betrogen
bewerben (sich)	*to apply for*	bewarb	beworben
biegen	*to bend*	bog	gebogen
binden	*to bind*	band	gebunden
bitten	*to ask*	bat	gebeten
bleiben	*to remain*	blieb	ist geblieben
brechen	*to break*	brach	gebrochen
entscheiden	*to decide*	entschied	entschieden
essen	*to eat*	aß	gegessen
fahren	*to drive, ride, go*	fuhr	ist gefahren
fallen	*to fall*	fiel	ist gefallen
fangen	*to catch*	fing	gefangen
finden	*to find*	fand	gefunden
fliegen	*to fly*	flog	ist geflogen
fliehen	*to flee*	floh	ist geflohen
fließen	*to flow*	floß	ist geflossen
geben	*to give*	gab	gegeben
gehen	*to go*	ging	ist gegangen
gelingen	*to succeed*	gelang	ist gelungen
geschehen	*to happen*	geschah	ist geschehen
gewinnen	*to win, gain*	gewann	gewonnen
gießen	*to pour*	goß	gegossen
halten	*to hold*	hielt	gehalten
hangen	*to hang (intr.)*	hing	gehangen
heißen	*to be named, called*	hieß	geheißen
helfen	*to help*	half	geholfen
kommen	*to come*	kam	ist gekommen
lassen	*to let*	ließ	gelassen
laufen	*to run*	lief	ist gelaufen
leiden	*to suffer*	litt	gelitten
leihen	*to lend, borrow*	lieh	geliehen
lesen	*to read*	las	gelesen
liegen	*to lie*	lag	gelegen
lügen	*to (tell a) lie*	log	gelogen
nehmen	*to take*	nahm	genommen

SYNOPSIS OF GRAMMAR

PRESENT INDICATIVE	PAST SUBJUNCTIVE	IMPERATIVE	INFINITIVE
er beginnt	begönne (or begänne)	beginn(e)	**beginnen**
er beißt	bisse	beiß(e)	**beißen**
er besinnt sich	besönne (or besänne)	besinne (dich)	**besinnen**
er betrügt	betröge	betrüg(e)	**betrügen**
er bewirbt sich	bewürbe	bewirb (dich)	**bewerben**
er biegt	böge	bieg(e)	**biegen**
er bindet	bände	bind(e)	**binden**
er bittet	bäte	bitt(e)	**bitten**
er bleibt	bliebe	bleib(e)	**bleiben**
er bricht	bräche	brich	**brechen**
er entscheidet	entschiede	entscheid(e)	**entscheiden**
er ißt	äße	iß	**essen**
er fährt	führe	fahr(e)	**fahren**
er fällt	fiele	fall(e)	**fallen**
er fängt	finge	fang(e)	**fangen**
er findet	fände	find(e)	**finden**
er fliegt	flöge	flieg(e)	**fliegen**
er flieht	flöhe	flieh(e)	**fliehen**
er fließt	flösse	fließ(e)	**fließen**
er gibt	gäbe	gib	**geben**
er geht	ginge	geh(e)	**gehen**
es gelingt	gelänge	—	**gelingen**
es geschieht	geschähe	—	**geschehen**
er gewinnt	gewönne (or gewänne)	gewinn(e)	**gewinnen**
er gießt	gösse	gieß(e)	**gießen**
er hält	hielte	halt(e)	**halten**
er hängt	hinge	hange	**hangen**
er heißt	hieße	heiß(e)	**heißen**
er hilft	hülfe (or hälfe)	hilf	**helfen**
er kommt	käme	komm(e)	**kommen**
er läßt	ließe	laß	**lassen**
er läuft	liefe	lauf(e)	**laufen**
er leidet	litte	leid(e)	**leiden**
er leiht	liehe	leih(e)	**leihen**
er liest	läse	lies	**lesen**
er liegt	läge	lieg(e)	**liegen**
er lügt	löge	lüg(e)	**lügen**
er nimmt	nähme	nimm	**nehmen**

INFINITIVE	MEANING	PAST INDICATIVE	PAST PARTICIPLE
raten	*to advise, guess*	riet	geraten
reißen	*to tear*	riß	gerissen
reiten	*to ride (on horseback)*	ritt	ist geritten
riechen	*to smell*	roch	gerochen
rufen	*to call*	rief	gerufen
scheinen	*to seem, shine*	schien	geschienen
schelten	*to scold*	schalt	gescholten
schlafen	*to sleep*	schlief	geschlafen
schlagen	*to strike*	schlug	geschlagen
schließen	*to close*	schloß	geschlossen
schneiden	*to cut*	schnitt	geschnitten
schreiben	*to write*	schrieb	geschrieben
schreien	*to scream*	schrie	geschrie(e)n
schweigen	*to be silent*	schwieg	geschwiegen
schwimmen	*to swim*	schwamm	ist geschwommen
schwinden	*to vanish* (verschwinden)	schwand	ist geschwunden
sehen	*to see*	sah	gesehen
sein	*to be*	war	ist gewesen
singen	*to sing*	sang	gesungen
sitzen	*to sit*	saß	gesessen
sprechen	*to speak*	sprach	gesprochen
springen	*to jump*	sprang	ist gesprungen
stehen	*to stand*	stand	gestanden
stehlen	*to steal*	stahl	gestohlen
steigen	*to climb*	stieg	ist gestiegen
sterben	*to die*	starb	ist gestorben
stoßen	*to push*	stieß	gestoßen
streichen	*to stroke, paint*	strich	gestrichen
tragen	*to carry*	trug	getragen
treffen	*to meet, hit*	traf	getroffen
treten	*to step*	trat	ist getreten
trinken	*to drink*	trank	getrunken
tun	*to do*	tat	getan
vergessen	*to forget*	vergaß	vergessen
verlieren	*to lose*	verlor	verloren
wachsen	*to grow*	wuchs	ist gewachsen
waschen	*to wash*	wusch	gewaschen
weisen	*to show*	wies	gewiesen
werden	*to become*	wurde	ist geworden
werfen	*to throw*	warf	geworfen
ziehen*	*to pull*	zog	gezogen

* As an intransitive verb, **ziehen** (*to move*) is conjugated with **sein.**

PRESENT INDICATIVE	PAST SUBJUNCTIVE	IMPERATIVE	INFINITIVE
er rät	riete	rat(e)	**raten**
er reißt	risse	reiß(e)	**reißen**
er reitet	ritte	reit(e)	**reiten**
er riecht	röche	riech(e)	**riechen**
er ruft	riefe	ruf(e)	**rufen**
er scheint	schiene	schein(e)	**scheinen**
er schilt	schölte (or schälte)	schilt	**schelten**
er schläft	schliefe	schlaf(e)	**schlafen**
er schlägt	schlüge	schlag(e)	**schlagen**
er schließt	schlösse	schließ(e)	**schließen**
er schneidet	schnitte	schneid(e)	**schneiden**
er schreibt	schriebe	schreib(e)	**schreiben**
er schreit	schriee	schrei(e)	**schreien**
er schweigt	schwiege	schweig(e)	**schweigen**
er schwimmt	schwömme (or schwämme)	schwimm(e)	**schwimmen**
er schwindet	schwände	schwind(e)	**schwinden**
er sieht	sähe	sieh	**sehen**
er ist	wäre	sei	**sein**
er singt	sänge	sing(e)	**singen**
er sitzt	säße	sitz(e)	**sitzen**
er spricht	spräche	sprich	**sprechen**
er springt	spränge	spring(e)	**springen**
er steht	stände (or stünde)	steh(e)	**stehen**
er stiehlt	stöhle (or stähle)	stiehl	**stehlen**
er steigt	stiege	steig(e)	**steigen**
er stirbt	stürbe	stirb	**sterben**
er stößt	stieße	stoß(e)	**stoßen**
er streicht	striche	streich(e)	**streichen**
er trägt	trüge	trag(e)	**tragen**
er trifft	träfe	triff	**treffen**
er tritt	träte	tritt	**treten**
er trinkt	tränke	trink(e)	**trinken**
er tut	täte	tu(e)	**tun**
er vergißt	vergäße	vergiß	**vergessen**
er verliert	verlöre	verlier(e)	**verlieren**
er wächst	wüchse	wachse	**wachsen**
er wäscht	wüsche	wasch(e)	**waschen**
er weist	wiese	weise	**weisen**
er wird	würde	werd(e)	**werden**
er wirft	würfe	wirf	**werfen**
er zieht	zöge	zieh(e)	**ziehen***

2 · Irregular Weak Verbs

INFINITIVE	MEANING	PAST INDICATIVE	PAST PARTICIPLE
brennen	*to burn*	brannte	gebrannt
— kennen	*to know*	kannte	gekannt
nennen	*to name*	nannte	genannt
rennen	*to run*	rannte	ist gerannt *
senden	*to send*	sandte	gesandt
denken	*to think*	dachte	gedacht
bringen	*to bring*	brachte	gebracht
wissen	*to know*	wußte	gewußt

* Also transitive, **hat gerannt;** see p. 28.

PRESENT INDICATIVE	PAST SUBJUNCTIVE	IMPERATIVE	INFINITIVE
er brennt	brennte	brenn(e)	**brennen**
er kennt	kennte	kenn(e)	**kennen**
er nennt	nennte	nenn(e)	**nennen**
er rennt	rennte	renn(e)	**rennen**
er sendet	sendete	send(e)	**senden**
er denkt	dächte	denk(e)	**denken**
er bringt	brächte	bring(e)	**bringen**
er weiß	wüßte	wisse	**wissen** *

* Although not a modal auxiliary, **wissen** resembles one in the conjugation of its present indicative:

SINGULAR: ich weiß, du weißt, er weiß
PLURAL: wir wissen, ihr wißt, sie wissen

3 · Conjugation of __Haben__

Indicative	*Subjunctive*

PRESENT

I have

ich habe	ich habe
du hast	du habest
er hat	er habe
wir haben	wir haben
ihr habt	ihr habet
sie haben	sie haben

PRESENT PERFECT

I have had

ich habe gehabt	habe gehabt
du hast gehabt	habest gehabt
er hat gehabt	habe gehabt
wir haben gehabt	haben gehabt
ihr habt gehabt	habet gehabt
sie haben gehabt	haben gehabt

FUTURE

I shall have

ich werde haben	ich werde haben
du wirst haben	du werdest haben
er wird haben	er werde haben
wir werden haben	wir werden haben
ihr werdet haben	ihr werdet haben
sie werden haben	sie werden haben

•

Imperative

habe, habt, haben Sie, *have*

Infinitive

PRESENT INFINITIVE: haben, *to have*
PERFECT INFINITIVE: gehabt (zu) haben, *to have had*

Participle

PRESENT PARTICIPLE: habend, *having*
PERFECT PARTICIPLE: gehabt, *had*

Indicative	*Subjunctive*

PAST

I had

ich hatte	ich hätte
du hattest	du hättest
er hatte	er hätte
wir hatten	wir hätten
ihr hattet	ihr hättet
sie hatten	sie hätten

PAST PERFECT

I had had

hatte gehabt	hätte gehabt
hattest gehabt	hättest gehabt
hatte gehabt	hätte gehabt
hatten gehabt	hätten gehabt
hattet gehabt	hättet gehabt
hatten gehabt	hätten gehabt

FUTURE PERFECT

I shall have had

ich werde gehabt haben	ich werde gehabt haben
du wirst gehabt haben	du werdest gehabt haben
er wird gehabt haben	er werde gehabt haben
wir werden gehabt haben	wir werden gehabt haben
ihr werdet gehabt haben	ihr werdet gehabt haben
sie werden gehabt haben	sie werden gehabt haben

PRESENT CONDITIONAL

I should have

PAST CONDITIONAL

I should have had

ich würde haben	ich würde gehabt haben
du würdest haben	du würdest gehabt haben
er würde haben	er würde gehabt haben
wir würden haben	wir würden gehabt haben
ihr würdet haben	ihr würdet gehabt haben
sie würden haben	sie würden gehabt haben

4 · Conjugation of Sein

Indicative	*Subjunctive*

PRESENT

I am (be)

ich bin	ich sei
du bist	du seiest
er ist	er sei
wir sind	wir seien
ihr seid	ihr seiet
sie sind	sie seien

PRESENT PERFECT

I have been

ich bin gewesen	sei gewesen
du bist gewesen	seiest gewesen
er ist gewesen	sei gewesen
wir sind gewesen	seien gewesen
ihr seid gewesen	seiet gewesen
sie sind gewesen	seien gewesen

FUTURE

I shall be

ich werde sein	ich werde sein
du wirst sein	du werdest sein
er wird sein	er werde sein
wir werden sein	wir werden sein
ihr werdet sein	ihr werdet sein
sie werden sein	sie werden sein

●

Imperative

sei, seid, seien Sie, *be*

Infinitive

PRESENT INFINITIVE: sein, *to be*
PERFECT INFINITIVE: gewesen (zu) sein, *to have been*

Participle

PRESENT PARTICIPLE: seiend, *being*
PERFECT PARTICIPLE: gewesen, *been*

Indicative	Subjunctive

PAST

I was (were)

ich war	ich wäre
du warst	du wärest
er war	er wäre
wir waren	wir wären
ihr wart	ihr wäret
sie waren	sie wären

PAST PERFECT

I had been

war gewesen	wäre gewesen
warst gewesen	wärest gewesen
war gewesen	wäre gewesen
waren gewesen	wären gewesen
wart gewesen	wäret gewesen
waren gewesen	wären gewesen

FUTURE PERFECT

I shall have been

ich werde gewesen sein	ich werde gewesen sein
du wirst gewesen sein	du werdest gewesen sein
er wird gewesen sein	er werde gewesen sein
wir werden gewesen sein	wir werden gewesen sein
ihr werdet gewesen sein	ihr werdet gewesen sein
sie werden gewesen sein	sie werden gewesen sein

•

PRESENT CONDITIONAL

I should be

ich würde sein
du würdest sein
er würde sein
wir würden sein
ihr würdet sein
sie würden sein

PAST CONDITIONAL

I should have been

ich würde gewesen sein
du würdest gewesen sein
er würde gewesen sein
wir würden gewesen sein
ihr würdet gewesen sein
sie würden gewesen sein

5 · Conjugation of <u>Werden</u>

<table>
<tr><td>Indicative</td><td></td><td>Subjunctive</td></tr>
</table>

PRESENT

I become

ich werde	ich werde
du wirst	du werdest
er wird	er werde
wir werden	wir werden
ihr werdet	ihr werdet
sie werden	sie werden

PRESENT PERFECT

I have become

ich bin geworden	sei geworden
du bist geworden	seiest geworden
er ist geworden	sei geworden
wir sind beworden	seien geworden
ihr seid geworden	seiet geworden
sie sind geworden	seien geworden

FUTURE

I shall become

ich werde werden	ich werde werden
du wirst werden	du werdest werden
er wird werden	er werde werden
wir werden werden	wir werden werden
ihr werdet werden	ihr werdet werden
sie werden werden	sie werden werden

•

Imperative

werde, werdet, werden Sie, *become*

Infinitive

PRESENT INFINITIVE: werden, *to become*
PERFECT INFINITIVE: geworden (zu) sein, *to have become*

Participle

PRESENT PARTICIPLE: werdend, *becoming*
PERFECT PARTICIPLE: geworden, *become*

Indicative	*Subjunctive*

PAST

I became

ich wurde	ich würde
du wurdest	du würdest
er wurde	er würde
wir wurden	wir würden
ihr wurdet	ihr würdet
sie wurden	sie würden

PAST PERFECT

I had become

war geworden	wäre geworden
warst geworden	wärest geworden
war geworden	wäre geworden
waren geworden	wären geworden
wart geworden	wäret geworden
waren geworden	wären geworden

FUTURE PERFECT

I shall have become

ich werde geworden sein	ich werde geworden sein
du wirst geworden sein	du werdest geworden sein
er wird geworden sein	er werde geworden sein
wir werden geworden sein	wir werden geworden sein
ihr werdet geworden sein	ihr werdet geworden sein
sie werden geworden sein	sie werden geworden sein

●

PRESENT CONDITIONAL	PAST CONDITIONAL
I should become	*I should have become*
ich würde werden	ich würde geworden sein
du würdest werden	du würdest geworden sein
er würde werden	er würde geworden sein
wir würden werden	wir würden geworden sein
ihr würdet werden	ihr würdet geworden sein
sie würden werden	sie würden geworden sein

6 · Conjugation of Weak Verbs

Indicative		*Subjunctive*

PRESENT

I praise

ich lobe		ich lobe
du lobst		du lobest
er lobt		er lobe
wir loben		wir loben
ihr lobt		ihr lobet
sie loben		sie loben

PRESENT PERFECT

I have praised

ich habe gelobt		habe gelobt
du hast gelobt		habest gelobt
er hat gelobt		habe gelobt
wir haben gelobt		haben gelobt
ihr habt gelobt		habet gelobt
sie haben gelobt		haben gelobt

FUTURE

I shall praise

ich werde loben		ich werde loben
du wirst loben		du werdest loben
er wird loben		er werde loben
wir werden loben		wir werden loben
ihr werdet loben		ihr werdet loben
sie werden loben		sie werden loben

●

Imperative

lobe, lobt, loben Sie, *praise*

Infinitive

PRESENT INFINITIVE: loben, *to praise*
PERFECT INFINITIVE: gelobt (zu) haben, *to have praised*

Participle

PRESENT PARTICIPLE: lobend, *praising*
PERFECT PARTICIPLE: gelobt, *praised*

Indicative	Subjunctive

PAST

I praised

ich lobte	ich lobte
du lobtest	du lobtest
er lobte	er lobte
wir lobten	wir lobten
ihr lobtet	ihr lobtet
sie lobten	sie lobten

PAST PERFECT

I had praised

hatte gelobt	hätte gelobt
hattest gelobt	hättest gelobt
hatte gelobt	hätte gelobt
hatten gelobt	hätten gelobt
hattet gelobt	hättet gelobt
hatten gelobt	hätten gelobt

FUTURE PERFECT

I shall have praised

ich werde gelobt haben	ich werde gelobt haben
du wirst gelobt haben	du werdest gelobt haben
er wird gelobt haben	er werde gelobt haben
wir werden gelobt haben	wir werden gelobt haben
ihr werdet gelobt haben	ihr werdet gelobt haben
sie werden gelobt haben	sie werden gelobt haben

●

PRESENT CONDITIONAL	PAST CONDITIONAL
I should praise	*I should have praised*
ich würde loben	ich würde gelobt haben
du würdest loben	du würdest gelobt haben
er würde loben	er würde gelobt haben
wir würden loben	wir würden gelobt haben
ihr würdet loben	ihr würdet gelobt haben
sie würden loben	sie würden gelobt haben

7 · Conjugation of Strong Verbs

Indicative		*Subjunctive*

PRESENT

I sing

ich singe	ich singe
du singst	du singest
er singt	er singe
wir singen	wir singen
ihr singt	ihr singet
sie singen	sie singen

PRESENT PERFECT

I have sung

ich habe gesungen	habe gesungen
du hast gesungen	habest gesungen
er hat gesungen	habe gesungen
wir haben gesungen	haben gesungen
ihr habt gesungen	habet gesungen
sie haben gesungen	haben gesungen

FUTURE

I shall sing

ich werde singen	ich werde singen
du wirst singen	du werdest singen
er wird singen	er werde singen
wir werden singen	wir werden singen
ihr werdet singen	ihr werdet singen
sie werden singen	sie werden singen

●

Imperative

singe, singt, singen Sie, *sing*

Infinitive

PRESENT INFINITIVE: singen, *to sing*
PERFECT INFINITIVE: gesungen (zu) haben, *to have sung*

Participle

PRESENT PARTICIPLE: singend, *singing*
PERFECT PARTICIPLE: gesungen, *sung*

Indicative	*Subjunctive*

PAST

I sang

ich sang	ich sänge
du sangst	du sängest
er sang	er sänge
wir sangen	wir sängen
ihr sangt	ihr sänget
sie sangen	sie sängen

PAST PERFECT

I had sung

hatte gesungen	hätte gesungen
hattest gesungen	hättest gesungen
hatte gesungen	hätte gesungen
hatten gesungen	hätten gesungen
hattet gesungen	hättet gesungen
hatten gesungen	hätten gesungen

FUTURE PERFECT

I shall have sung

ich werde gesungen haben	ich werde gesungen haben
du wirst gesungen haben	du werdest gesungen haben
er wird gesungen haben	er werde gesungen haben
wir werden gesungen haben	wir werden gesungen haben
ihr werdet gesungen haben	ihr werdet gesungen haben
sie werden gesungen haben	sie werden gesungen haben

●

PRESENT CONDITIONAL	PAST CONDITIONAL
I should sing	*I should have sung*
ich würde singen	ich würde gesungen haben
du würdest singen	du würdest gesungen haben
er würde singen	er würde gesungen haben
wir würden singen	wir würden gesungen haben
ihr würdet singen	ihr würdet gesungen haben
sie würden singen	sie würden gesungen haben

8 · Passive Voice

Indicative	*Subjunctive*

I am praised

ich werde gelobt	ich werde gelobt
du wirst gelobt	du werdest gelobt
er wird gelobt	er werde gelobt
wir werden gelobt	wir werden gelobt
ihr werdet gelobt	ihr werdet gelobt
sie werden gelobt	sie werden gelobt

PRESENT PERFECT

I have been praised

ich bin gelobt worden	ich sei gelobt worden
du bist gelobt worden	du seiest gelobt worden
er ist gelobt worden	er sei gelobt worden
wir sind gelobt worden	wir seien gelobt worden
ihr seid gelobt worden	ihr seiet gelobt worden
sie sind gelobt worden	sie seien gelobt worden

FUTURE

I shall be praised

ich werde gelobt werden	ich werde gelobt werden
du wirst gelobt werden	du werdest gelobt werden
er wird gelobt werden	er werde gelobt werden
wir werden gelobt werden	wir werden gelobt werden
ihr werdet gelobt werden	ihr werdet gelobt werden
sie werden gelobt werden	sie werden gelobt werden

●

Imperative

werde gelobt, werdet gelobt, werden Sie gelobt, *be praised*

Infinitive

PRESENT INFINITIVE: gelobt (zu) werden, *to be praised*
PERFECT INFINITIVE: gelobt worden (zu) sein, *to have been praised*

Participle

PRESENT PARTICIPLE: wanting.
PERFECT PARTICIPLE: gelobt worden, *been praised*

TABOR COLLEGE LIBRARY
Hillsboro, Kansas 67063

Indicative	*Subjunctive*

PAST

I was praised

ich wurde gelobt	ich würde gelobt
du wurdest gelobt	du würdest gelobt
er wurde gelobt	er würde gelobt
wir wurden gelobt	wir würden gelobt
ihr wurdet gelobt	ihr würdet gelobt
sie wurden gelobt	sie würden gelobt

PAST PERFECT

I had been praised

ich war gelobt worden	ich wäre gelobt worden
du warst gelobt worden	du wärest gelobt worden
er war gelobt worden	er wäre gelobt worden
wir waren gelobt worden	wir wären gelobt worden
ihr wart gelobt worden	ihr wäret gelobt worden
sie waren gelobt worden	sie wären gelobt worden

FUTURE PERFECT

I shall have been praised

ich werde gelobt worden sein	ich werde gelobt worden sein
du wirst gelobt worden sein	du werdest gelobt worden sein
er wird gelobt worden sein	er werde gelobt worden sein
wir werden gelobt worden sein	wir werden gelobt worden sein
ihr werdet gelobt worden sein	ihr werdet gelobt worden sein
sie werden gelobt worden sein	sie werden gelobt worden sein

●

PRESENT CONDITIONAL	PAST CONDITIONAL
I should be praised	*I should have been praised*
ich würde gelobt werden	ich würde gelobt worden sein
du würdest gelobt werden	du würdest gelobt worden sein
er würde gelobt werden	er würde gelobt worden sein
wir würden gelobt werden	wir würden gelobt worden sein
ihr würdet gelobt werden	ihr würdet gelobt worden sein
sie würden gelobt werden	sie würden gelobt worden sein

9 · Conjugation of Reflexive Verbs

Indicative	*Subjunctive*

I remember

ich erinnere mich	ich erinnere mich
du erinnerst dich	du erinnerest dich
er erinnert sich	er erinnere sich
wir erinnern uns	wir erinnern uns
ihr erinnert euch	ihr erinneret euch
sie erinnern sich	sie erinnern sich

PRESENT PERFECT

I have remembered

ich habe mich erinnert	ich habe mich erinnert
du hast dich erinnert	du habest dich erinnert
er hat sich erinnert	er habe sich erinnert
wir haben uns erinnert	wir haben uns erinnert
ihr habt euch erinnert	ihr habet euch erinnert
sie haben sich erinnert	sie haben sich erinnert

FUTURE

I shall remember

ich werde mich erinnern	ich werde mich erinnern
du wirst dich erinnern	du werdest dich erinnern
er wird sich erinnern	er werde sich erinnern
wir werden uns erinnern	wir werden uns erinnern
ihr werdet euch erinnern	ihr werdet euch erinnern
sie werden sich erinnern	sie werden sich erinnern

•

Imperative

erinnere dich, erinnert euch, erinnern Sie sich, *remember*

Infinitive

PRESENT INFINITIVE: sich (zu) erinnern, *to remember*
PERFECT INFINITIVE: sich erinnert (zu) haben, *to have remembered*

Participle

PRESENT PARTICIPLE: sich erinnernd, *remembering*
PERFECT PARTICIPLE: sich erinnert, *remembered*

Indicative	Subjunctive

PAST

I remembered

ich erinnerte mich	ich erinnerte mich
du erinnertest dich	du erinnertest dich
er erinnerte sich	er erinnerte sich
wir erinnerten uns	wir erinnerten uns
ihr erinnertet euch	ihr erinnertet euch
sie erinnerten sich	sie erinnerten sich

PAST PERFECT

I had remembered

ich hatte mich erinnert	ich hätte mich erinnert
du hattest dich erinnert	du hättest dich erinnert
er hatte sich erinnert	er hätte sich erinnert
wir hatten uns erinnert	wir hätten uns erinnert
ihr hattet euch erinnert	ihr hättet euch erinnert
sie hatten sich erinnert	sie hätten sich erinnert

FUTURE PERFECT

I shall have remembered

ich werde mich erinnert haben	ich werde mich erinnert haben
du wirst dich erinnert haben	du werdest dich erinnert haben
er wird sich erinnert haben	er werde sich erinnert haben
wir werden uns erinnert haben	wir werden uns erinnert haben
ihr werdet euch erinnert haben	ihr werdet euch erinnert haben
sie werden sich erinnert haben	sie werden sich erinnert haben

●

PRESENT CONDITIONAL	PAST CONDITIONAL
I should remember	*I should have remembered*
ich würde mich erinnern	ich würde mich erinnert haben
du würdest dich erinnern	du würdest dich erinnert haben
er würde sich erinnern	er würde sich erinnert haben
wir würden uns erinnern	wir würden uns erinnert haben
ihr würdet euch erinnern	ihr würdet euch erinnert haben
sie würden sich erinnern	sie würden sich erinnert haben

10 · Modal Auxiliaries: <u>Dürfen, Können,</u> <u>Mögen, Müssen, Sollen, Wollen</u>

Indicative

PRESENT

ich	darf	kann	mag
du	darfst	kannst	magst
er	darf	kann	mag
wir	dürfen	können	mögen
ihr	dürft	könnt	mögt
sie	dürfen	können	mögen

PAST

ich	durfte	konnte	mochte
du	durftest	konntest	mochtest
er	durfte	konnte	mochte
wir	durften	konnten	mochten
ihr	durftet	konntet	mochtet
sie	durften	konnten	mochten

PRESENT PERFECT

ich habe	gedurft	gekonnt	gemocht
du hast	gedurft	gekonnt	gemocht
er hat	gedurft	gekonnt	gemocht
BUT:			
ich habe gehen	dürfen	können	mögen
du hast gehen	dürfen	können	mögen
er hat gehen	dürfen	können	mögen

PAST PERFECT

ich hatte	gedurft	gekonnt	gemocht
du hattest	gedurft	gekonnt	gemocht
er hatte	gedurft	gekonnt	gemocht
BUT:			
ich hatte gehen	dürfen	können	mögen
du hattest gehen	dürfen	können	mögen
er hatte gehen	dürfen	können	mögen

ich werde	dürfen	können	mögen
du wirst	dürfen	können	mögen
er wird	dürfen	können	mögen
wir werden	dürfen	können	mögen
ihr werdet	dürfen	können	mögen
sie werden	dürfen	können	mögen

FUTURE PERFECT

ich werde	gedurft	gekonnt	gemocht	**haben**
du wirst	gedurft	gekonnt	gemocht	**haben**
er wird	gedurft	gekonnt	gemocht	**haben**
BUT:				
ich werde haben gehen	dürfen	können	mögen	
du wirst haben gehen	dürfen	können	mögen	
er wird haben gehen	dürfen	können	mögen	

Infinitive

PRESENT:	dürfen	können	mögen
PERFECT:	{ gedurft	gekonnt	gemocht
	{ haben	haben	haben

Participle

PRESENT PARTICIPLE:	dürfend	könnend	mögend
PAST PARTICIPLE:	{ gedurft	gekonnt	gemocht
	{ dürfen	können	mögen

Subjunctive

ich	dürfe	könne	möge
du	dürfest	könnest	mögest
er	dürfe	könne	möge
wir	dürfen	können	mögen
ihr	dürfet	könnet	möget
sie	dürfen	können	mögen

PAST

ich	dürfte	könnte	möchte
du	dürftest	könntest	möchtest
er	dürfte	könnte	möchte
wir	dürften	könnten	möchten
ihr	dürftet	könntet	möchtet
sie	dürften	könnten	möchten

PRESENT PERFECT

ich habe	gedurft	gekonnt	gemocht
du habest	gedurft	gekonnt	gemocht
er habe	gedurft	gekonnt	gemocht
BUT:			
ich habe gehen	dürfen	können	mögen
du habest gehen	dürfen	können	mögen
er habe gehen	dürfen	können	mögen

PAST PERFECT

ich hätte	gedurft	gekonnt	gemocht
du hättest	gedurft	gekonnt	gemocht
er hätte	gedurft	gekonnt	gemocht
BUT:			
ich hätte gehen	dürfen	können	mögen
du hättest gehen	dürfen	können	mögen
er hätte gehen	dürfen	können	mögen

ich werde	dürfen	können	mögen
du werdest	dürfen	können	mögen
er werde	dürfen	können	mögen
wir werden	dürfen	können	mögen
ihr werdet	dürfen	können	mögen
sie werden	dürfen	können	mögen

FUTURE PERFECT

ich werde	gedurft	gekonnt	gemocht	haben
du werdest	gedurft	gekonnt	gemocht	haben
er werde	gedurft	gekonnt	gemocht	haben

BUT:

ich werde haben gehen	dürfen	können	mögen
du werdest haben gehen	dürfen	können	mögen
er werde haben gehen	dürfen	können	mögen

Conditional

PRESENT

ich würde	dürfen	können	mögen
du würdest	dürfen	können	mögen
er würde	dürfen	können	mögen

PAST

ich würde	gedurft	gekonnt	gemocht	haben
du würdest	gedurft	gekonnt	gemocht	haben
er würde	gedurft	gekonnt	gemocht	haben

BUT:

ich würde haben gehen	dürfen	können	mögen
du würdest haben gehen	dürfen	können	mögen
er würde haben gehen	dürfen	können	mögen

Modal Auxiliaries: <u>Müssen, Sollen, Wollen</u>

Indicative

ich	muß	soll	will
du	mußt	sollst	willst
er	muß	soll	will
wir	müssen	sollen	wollen
ihr	müßt	sollt	wollt
sie	müssen	sollen	wollen

PAST

ich	mußte	sollte	wollte
du	mußtest	solltest	wolltest
er	mußte	sollte	wollte
wir	mußten	sollten	wollten
ihr	mußtet	solltet	wolltet
sie	mußten	sollten	wollten

PRESENT PERFECT

ich habe	gemußt	gesollt	gewollt
du hast	gemußt	gesollt	gewollt
er hat	gemußt	gesollt	gewollt

BUT:

ich habe gehen	müssen	sollen	wollen
du hast gehen	müssen	sollen	wollen
er hat gehen	müssen	sollen	wollen

PAST PERFECT

ich hatte	gemußt	gesollt	gewollt
du hattest	gemußt	gesollt	gewollt
er hatte	gemußt	gesollt	gewollt

BUT:

ich hatte gehen	müssen	sollen	wollen
du hattest gehen	müssen	sollen	wollen
er hatte gehen	müssen	sollen	wollen

FUTURE

ich werde	müssen	sollen	wollen
du wirst	müssen	sollen	wollen
er wird	müssen	sollen	wollen
wir werden	müssen	sollen	wollen
ihr werdet	müssen	sollen	wollen
sie werden	müssen	sollen	wollen

SYNOPSIS OF GRAMMAR

ich werde	gemußt	gesollt	gewollt	**haben**
du wirst	gemußt	gesollt	gewollt	**haben**
er wird	gemußt	gesollt	gewollt	**haben**

BUT:

ich werde haben gehen	müssen	sollen	wollen
du wirst haben gehen	müssen	sollen	wollen
er wird haben gehen	müssen	sollen	wollen

INFINITIVE

PRESENT:	müssen	sollen	wollen
PERFECT:	{gemußt {haben	{gesollt {haben	{gewollt {haben

PARTICIPLE

PRESENT PARTICIPLE:	müssend	sollend	wollend
PAST PARTICIPLE:	{gemußt {müssen	{gesollt {sollen	{gewollt {wollen

Subjunctive:

	PRESENT		
ich	müsse	solle	wolle
du	müssest	sollest	wollest
er	müsse	solle	wolle
wir	müssen	sollen	wollen
ihr	müsset	sollet	wollet
sie	müssen	sollen	wollen

	PAST		
ich	müßte	sollte	wollte
du	müßtest	solltest	wolltest
er	müßte	sollte	wollte
wir	müßten	sollten	wollten
ihr	müßtet	solltet	wollten
sie	müßten	sollten	wollten

	PRESENT PERFECT		
ich habe	gemußt	gesollt	gewollt
du habest	gemußt	gesollt	gewollt
er habe	gemußt	gesollt	gewollt

BUT:

ich habe gehen	müssen	sollen	wollen
du habest gehen	müssen	sollen	wollen
er habe gehen	müssen	sollen	wollen

	PAST PERFECT		
ich hätte	gemußt	gesollt	gewollt
du hättest	gemußt	gesollt	gewollt
er hätte	gemußt	gesollt	gewollt

BUT:

ich hätte gehen	müssen	sollen	wollen
du hättest gehen	müssen	sollen	wollen
er hätte gehen	müssen	sollen	wollen

	FUTURE		
ich werde	müssen	sollen	wollen
du werdest	müssen	sollen	wollen
er werde	müssen	sollen	wollen
wir werden	müssen	sollen	wollen
ihr werdet	müssen	sollen	wollen
sie werden	müssen	sollen	wollen

ich werde	gemußt	gesollt	gewollt	**haben**
du werdest	gemußt	gesollt	gewollt	**haben**
er werde	gemußt	gesollt	gewollt	**haben**

BUT:

ich werde haben gehen	müssen	sollen	wollen
du werdest haben gehen	müssen	sollen	wollen
er werde haben gehen	müssen	sollen	wollen

Conditional

PRESENT

ich würde	müssen	sollen	wollen
du würdest	müssen	sollen	wollen
er würde	müssen	sollen	wollen

PAST

ich würde	gemußt	gesollt	gewollt	**haben**
du würdest	gemußt	gesollt	gewollt	**haben**
er würde	gemußt	gesollt	gewollt	**haben**

BUT:

ich würde haben gehen	müssen	sollen	wollen
du würdest haben gehen	müssen	sollen	wollen
er würde haben gehen	müssen	sollen	wollen

CLASS I: STRONG DECLENSION

			SINGULAR	
N.	der Bruder	der Onkel	die Mutter	das Gebäude
G.	des Bruders	des Onkels	der Mutter	des Gebäudes
D.	dem Bruder	dem Onkel	der Mutter	dem Gebäude
A.	den Bruder	den Onkel	die Mutter	das Gebäude
			PLURAL	
N.	die Brüder	die Onkel	die Mütter	die Gebäude
G.	der Brüder	der Onkel	der Mütter	der Gebäude
D.	den Brüdern	den Onkeln	den Müttern	den Gebäuden
A.	die Brüder	die Onkel	die Mütter	die Gebäude

To the first class of strong declension (no plural ending added) belong: 1) The masculines and neuters in -el, -er, -en (der Nagel, der Schlüssel, der Apfel, der Mantel, das Mittel, der Winter, der Dichter, der Lehrer, das Zimmer, das Messer, der Regen, der Garten, der Ofen, das Essen, das Leben, etc.); 2) The two feminines die Mutter, die Tochter; 3) The diminutives in -chen and -lein (das Mädchen, das Häuschen, das Fräulein, das Vöglein, das Wäglein, etc.); 4) The neuters with the prefix Ge- and the suffix -e (das Gebäude, das Gebirge, das Gemälde, etc.). Umlaut: Masculines often, feminines always, neuters never (except das Kloster, pl. die Klöster).

CLASS II: STRONG DECLENSION

	SINGULAR			
N.	der Kopf	der Tag	die Nacht	das Jahr
G.	des Kopfes	des Tages	der Nacht	des Jahres
D.	dem Kopf(e)	dem Tag(e)	der Nacht	dem Jahr(e)
A.	den Kopf	den Tag	die Nacht	das Jahr
	PLURAL			
N.	die Köpfe	die Tage	die Nächte	die Jahre
G.	der Köpfe	der Tage	der Nächte	der Jahre
D.	den Köpfen	den Tagen	den Nächten	den Jahren
A.	die Köpfe	die Tage	die Nächte	die Jahre

To the second class of strong declension (plural ending -e) belong: 1. Many masculines, feminines, and neuters of one syllable; 2. Nouns in **-sal, -nis, -kunft, -ig, -ling, -ing** (**das Schicksal, das Gefängnis, die Ankunft, der Pfennig, der Frühling, der Hering,** etc.); 3. A number of polysyllabic masculines and neuters (**der Monat, das Papier, das Dutzend,** etc.); Umlaut: Masculines often, feminines always, neuters never.

CLASS III: STRONG DECLENSION

	SINGULAR			
N.	das Haus	der Mann	das Königtum	der Irrtum
G.	des Hauses	des Mannes	des Königtums	des Irrtums
D.	dem Haus(e)	dem Mann(e)	dem Königtum	dem Irrtum
A.	das Haus	den Mann	das Königtum	den Irrtum
	PLURAL			
N.	die Häuser	die Männer	die Königtümer	die Irrtümer
G.	der Häuser	der Männer	der Königtümer	der Irrtümer
D.	den Häusern	den Männern	den Königtümern	den Irrtümern
A.	die Häuser	die Männer	die Königtümer	die Irrtümer

To the third class of the strong declension (plural ending -er) belong: 1. The most common monosyllabic neuters; 2. A few masculines of one syllable (**der Mann, der Ort, der Wald, der Leib, der Geist,** etc.); 3. All neuter or masculine nouns in **-tum** (**das Eigentum, das Königtum, der Irrtum, der Reichtum,** etc.)

	SINGULAR			
N.	der Knabe	der Mensch	die Frage	die Freundin
G.	des Knaben	des Menschen	der Frage	der Freundin
D.	dem Knaben	dem Menschen	der Frage	der Freundin
A.	den Knaben	den Menschen	die Frage	die Freundin
	PLURAL			
N.	die Knaben	die Menschen	die Fragen	die Freundinnen
G.	der Knaben	der Menschen	der Fragen	der Freundinnen
D.	den Knaben	den Menschen	den Fragen	den Freundinnen
A.	die Knaben	die Menschen	die Fragen	die Freundinnen

To the weak declension (plural ending -n or -en*) belong: 1. All the feminines that do not belong to class I or II strong declension; 2. A few masculines of one syllable denoting living beings (**der Mensch, der Narr, der Hirt, der Graf,** etc.); 3. A number of masculines of more than one syllable denoting living beings (**der Junge, der Knabe, der Bursche, der Löwe, der Neffe, der Soldat, der Student,** etc.). Umlaut: Never.

MIXED DECLENSION OF NOUNS

	SINGULAR			
N.	der Schmerz	der Nachbar	der Doktor	das Auge
G.	des Schmerzes	des Nachbars	des Doktors	des Auges
D.	dem Schmerz	dem Nachbar	dem Doktor	dem Auge
A.	den Schmerz	den Nachbar	den Doktor	das Auge
	PLURAL			
N.	die Schmerzen	die Nachbarn	die Doktoren	die Augen
G.	der Schmerzen	der Nachbarn	der Doktoren	der Augen
D.	den Schmerzen	den Nachbarn	den Doktoren	den Augen
A.	die Schmerzen	die Nachbarn	die Doktoren	die Augen

To the mixed declension (genitive sing. —s or —es, pl. —n or —en) belong: 1. A small number of masculines and neuters (**der Bauer, der See, der Staat, das Bett, das Ende, das Ohr,** etc.); 2. Foreign words in —or (**der Doktor, der Professor,** etc.). Umlaut: Never.

* Nouns ending in -in double the -n- before the ending: **die Freundin, die Freundinnen; die Lehrerin, die Lehrerinnen; die Studentin, die Studentinnen.**

260

	SINGULAR			
N.	der Friede(n)	der Name(n)	das Herz	der Herr
G.	des Friedens	des Namens	des Herzens	des Herrn
D.	dem Frieden	dem Namen	dem Herz	dem Herrn
A.	den Frieden	den Namen	das Herz	den Herrn
	PLURAL			
N.	die Frieden	die Namen	die Herzen	die Herren
G.	der Frieden	der Namen	der Herzen	der Herren
D.	den Frieden	den Namen	den Herzen	den Herren
A.	die Frieden	die Namen	die Herzen	die Herren

To this group of variants of unchanged plurals, -en plurals, and genitive -es belong: 1. A small number of masculine nouns: (**der Funke(n), die Funken; der Glaube(n)**, no plural; **der Same(n), die Samen; der Wille(n), die Willen; der Gedanke(n), die Gedanken; der Haufe(n), die Haufen; der Schade(n), die Schäden**); 2. The neuter: **das Herz.** Umlaut: Never.

STRONG DECLENSION OF ADJECTIVES

	SINGULAR		
	Masculine	*Feminine*	*Neuter*
N.	stark**er** Kaffee	rot**e** Kreide	kalt**es** Wasser
G.	stark**en** Kaffees	rot**er** Kreide	kalt**en** Wassers
D.	stark**em** Kaffee	rot**er** Kreide	kalt**em** Wasser
A.	stark**en** Kaffee	rot**e** Kreide	kalt**es** Wasser
	PLURAL		
N.	treu**e** Freunde	gut**e** Frauen	schön**e** Länder
G.	treu**er** Freunde	gut**er** Frauen	schön**er** Länder
D.	treu**en** Freunden	gut**en** Frauen	schön**en** Ländern
A.	treu**e** Freunde	gut**e** Frauen	schön**e** Länder

WEAK DECLENSION OF ADJECTIVES

*(Adjective preceded by a **der**-word)*

	SINGULAR		
	Masculine	*Feminine*	*Neuter*
N.	der kalte Winter	diese gute Mutter	jenes große Haus
G.	des kalten Winters	dieser guten Mutter	jenes großen Hauses
D.	dem kalten Winter	dieser guten Mutter	jenem großen Haus
A.	den kalten Winter	diese gute Mutter	jenes große Haus
	PLURAL		
N.	die kalten Winter	diese guten Mütter	jene großen Häuser
G.	der kalten Winter	dieser guten Mütter	jener großen Häuser
D.	den kalten Wintern	diesen guten Müttern	jenen großen Häusern
A.	die kalten Winter	diese guten Mütter	jene großen Häuser

MIXED DECLENSION OF ADJECTIVES

*(Adjective preceded by an **ein**-word)*

	SINGULAR	
	Masculine	*Feminine*
N.	kein hoher Berg	meine kleine Schwester
G.	keines hohen Berges	meiner kleinen Schwester
D.	keinem hohen Berg	meiner kleinen Schwester
A.	keinen hohen Berg	meine kleine Schwester

Neuter

sein kleines Zimmer
seines kleinen Zimmers
seinem kleinen Zimmer
sein kleines Zimmer

	PLURAL	
N.	keine hohen Berge	meine kleinen Schwestern
G.	keiner hohen Berge	meiner kleinen Schwestern
D.	keinen hohen Bergen	meinen kleinen Schwestern
A.	keine hohen Berge	meine kleinen Schwestern

seine kleinen Zimmer
seiner kleinen Zimmer
seinen kleinen Zimmern
seine kleinen Zimmer

VOCABULARIES

ABBREVIATIONS

acc.	accusative	*neut.*	neuter
adj.	adjective	*o. p.*	of person
adv.	adverb	*o. s.*	oneself
aux.	auxiliary	*pers.*	personal
dat.	dative	*p. p.*	past participle
def. art.	definite article	*pl.*	plural
fem.	feminine	*poss.*	possessive
fut.	future	*pref.*	prefix
gen.	genitive	*prep.*	preposition
imper.	imperative	*pron.*	pronoun
indef.	indefinite	*refl.*	reflexive
interr.	interrogative	*rel.*	relative
masc.	masculine	*sep.*	separable
mod.	modal	*sing.*	singular

NOTES ON THE VOCABULARIES

These vocabularies aim to be complete, the numerals, however, are omitted.

NOUNS: The nominative singular and plural of nouns are indicated. Where necessary or advisable to avoid confusion the genitive singular is also given.

VERBS: For ready reference, the principal parts of certain verbs are included in the vocabularies. Compound verbs with a separable prefix are designated by the use of hyphen (**an-kommen**).
An asterisk following the infinitive of a compound verb (**an-kommen***) indicates that the principal parts are listed under the simple verb.
The infinitive form of verbs that may be used reflexively is preceded by **sich.**
Verbs that govern the dative case are followed by *dat. of pers.*

ADJECTIVES: Umlaut in the comparative and superlative is indicated.

PREPOSITIONS: The case, or cases, governed by prepositions are indicated by *gen., dat., acc.,* or *dat. or acc.*

German-English Vocabulary

A

ab *adv.* off, away; down
ab-biegen* to turn off
ab-brechen* to break off
der **Abend, -e** evening; **abends** in the evening; **heute abend** tonight; **eines Abends** one evening; **gestern abend** last night
das **Abendessen** supper
aber *conj.* but, however
abertausend thousands
ab-fahren* to leave, depart (by car, train, etc.)
abgelegen *adj.* remote, distant
der **Abglanz** reflection
ab-holen to call for
ab-reisen to leave; **die Abreise, -n** departure
ab-reißen* to tear down
absurd *adj.* foolish, contrary to reason
abwärts *adv.* downward
achten to respect; pay attention to, take care; **in acht nehmen** to be on guard, take care
ächten to outlaw
der **Acker, ⸗** acre, field
die **Adresse, -n** address
der **Advokat, -en, -en** advocate, lawyer
das **Afrika** Africa; **afrikanisch** *adj.* of Africa
all (aller, alle, alles) *adj. or pron.* all, everything, everybody; **das alles** all that; **von allem** from everything; **von allen** from everybody
allein *adj. and adv.* alone; *conj.* but
alleinig *adj.* exclusive, only
die **Angelegenheit, -en** concern, affair
allgemein *adv.* general, universal
als *conj.* when; *in comparison* as; *after comparative* than; **als ob, als wenn** as if; **als sonst** than usually
alt *adj.* old, ancient; **der Alte, -n, -n** old man; **die Alten** the old (nations)
an *prep. dat. or acc.* at, to, up, against, on

ander *adj.* other, different; **am andern Tag** next day
an-fangen* to begin, start, set about; der **Anfang, ⸗e** beginning **anfangs** *adv.* at first
an-fragen to ask, inquire
an-gehen* to concern; **es geht mich nichts an** it is nothing to me, not my concern; **wie geht's nur an** how is it only possible
angenehm *adj.* pleasant, nice
die **Anhöhe, -n** elevation, knoll
an-kommen* to arrive; **die Ankunft** arrival
an-nehmen* to accept; take interest in
an-rufen* to call (as by telephone)
an-sehen* to look at
anstatt *prep. gen.* instead of
an-stürmen to assail, attack (violently)
antworten to answer; **die Antwort, -en** answer, reply
an-wenden to apply, make use of; **die Anwendung, -en** application
die **Anzahl** number
an-zeigen to announce, advertise
an-zünden to light, start
der **Apfel, ⸗** apple
arabisch *adj.* Arabian
arbeiten to work; **die Arbeit, -en** work
der **Arbeiter, -** working man, laborer
sich **ärgern** to be (become) angry; **ärgerlich** *adj.* angry; **sich ärgern über** *with acc.* to be angry at
der **Arm, -e** arm
arm *adj.* **ärmer, am ärmsten** poor, in need; **die Armut** poverty
das **Armband, ⸗er** bracelet
der **Arzt, ⸗e** physician; **die Ärztin** woman physician
(das) **Asien** Asia
atmen to breathe
auch *conj. and adv.* also, too, even
auf *prep. dat. or acc.* on, upon, to, in, at, for; **aufs Land** to the country; **auf und ab** up and down, back and forth
die **Aufgabe, -n** lesson, assignment, exercise; task; business

auf-geben* to give up, resign
aufgeregt *adj.* excited, irritated; **die
Aufregung** excitement
sich **auf-halten*** to stay
auf-hören to stop
auf-nehmen to take up
auf-schließen* to unlock
auf-stehen* to get up, rise
auf-weisen to show; exhibit
das **Auge, -n** eye
der **Augenblick, -e** moment
augenblicklich *adv.* momentary, immediately, just now
aus *prep. dat.* out of, from; *adv.* out,
over, ended
der **Ausblick, -e** view
aus-brechen* to break out, escape
ausgedörrt *adj.* dried up, parched
aus-gehen* to go out; end
aus-ruhen to rest
aus-sehen* to look, appear; **wie
sehen Sie aus!** how do you look!
außerhalb *prep. gen.* outside of
außerordentlich *adv.* extraordinary
die **Aussicht, -en** view
aus-treten* to trample out (fire)
auswendig *adv.* (to learn) by heart
das **Auto, -s, -s** auto, motor car
der **Autor, -s, -en** author

B

der **Bach, ⸗e** brook
bald *adv.* soon
der **Ball, ⸗e** ball
die **Ballade, -n** ballad
das **Band, ⸗er** ribbon
der **Band, ⸗e** volume
die **Bank, ⸗e** bench
die **Bank, -en** bank
der **Bär, -en** bear
der **Bau, -es, -ten** building, construction
bauen to build, construct
der **Bauer, -s, -n** peasant, farmer
der **Baum, ⸗e** tree
der **Beamte, -n, -n** official; public officer
beantworten to answer
bedenken* to consider, bear in mind
bedienen to serve; **die Bedienung**
service

beenden to finish, end
befehlen, befahl, befohlen, er befiehlt
to order, command; **der Befehl, -e**
order
befreien to free, liberate
begabt *adj.* gifted, talented; **die
Begabung, -en** talents
begegnen, ist begegnet *with dat. of
pers.* to meet
begehen to commit; celebrate
beginnen, begann, begonnen, er beginnt to begin, start
begleiten to accompany, escort; **der
Begleiter, -** companion
begraben* to bury
begrüßen to greet, welcome
behalten* to keep
behandeln to treat; **die Behandlung,
-en** treatment
behüten to protect
bei *prep. dat.* at, near, with, at the
home of; **bei uns** at our house, at
our place; **bei mir** with me; **bei
euch** at your place
beide *pron. and adj.* both, two; **alle
beide** both
das **Beispiel, -e** example; **zum Beispiel =
z. B.** for example
beißen, biß, gebissen, er beißt to bite
der **Beitrag, ⸗e** contribution
bekannt *adj.* known, well-known
bekommen* to get, receive ⸗
belebt *adj.* busy, bustling, crowded
beliebt *adj.* beloved, popular
belohnen to reward
bemerken to observe; remark
bemessen to measure; assign, allot
sich **bemühen** to try, endeavor
beneiden to envy
berauben to rob, deprive of
bereiten to prepare; cause
der **Berg, -e** hill, mountain
berichten to state, report; **der
Bericht, -e** report
berufen to call, appoint
berühmt *adj.* famous, distinguished,
celebrated
beschreiben* to describe; **die Beschreibung, -en** description
besitzen* to possess, own; **der
Besitzer, -** owner, occupant

besonders *adv.* especially, in particular
besser *adj.* better
die **Besserung** improvement; **gute Besserung!** a speedy recovery!
best- best; **aufs beste** in the best way; **zum Besten** for the benefit of; **am besten** the best
bestehen* to consist of; to pass (as an examination)
bestimmt *adv.* definitely, positively; to the point
bestrafen to punish
besuchen to visit; attend (school); der **Besuch, -e** visit; **einen Besuch machen** to pay a visit
beten to pray
betrachten to consider, regard
sich **betragen*** to behave; **das Betragen** behavior, conduct
betreffen, betraf, betroffen, es betrifft befall, fall upon, concern
das **Bett, -en** bed
bevor *conj.* before
bewahren to save, guard; **Gott bewahre!** God forbid!
beweisen, bewies, bewiesen, er beweist to prove, show; der **Beweis, -e** proof
bewohnen to inhabit; der **Bewohner, -** inhabitant, citizen
bewundern to admire
bezahlen to pay (for)
die **Bibel, -n** Bible
die **Bibliothek, -en** library
bieten, bot, geboten, er bietet to offer
das **Bild, -er** picture, painting
bilden to form; educate
billig *adj.* cheap
binden, band, gebunden, er bindet to tie, bind
bis *prep. and conj.* until; **bis an, bis zu** up to
bitten, bat, gebeten, er bittet to beg, request, ask (for something); **bitten um** ask for; **bitte!** please! die **Bitte, -n** request
bitter bitter; thoroughly
das **Blatt, ⸗er** leaf; sheet (of paper)
blau blue

bleiben, blieb, geblieben, er bleibt to stay, remain
der **Blick, -e** look, glance; view
blond *adj.* blond
blühen to bloom, blossom
die **Blume, -n** flower
(das) **Böhmen** Bohemia
(das) **Bonn:** city in West Germany
böse *adj.* angry; wicked; **das Böse** evil, bad
braten, briet, gebraten, er brät to roast, fry
brauchen to use, need
braun brown, tanned
brechen, brach, gebrochen, er bricht to break
(das) **Bremen:** name of a city, name of a ship
brennen, brannte, gebrannt, er brennt to burn; der **Brand, ⸗e** fire
der **Brief, -e** letter
der **Briefkasten, ⸗** letter box
die **Briefmarke, -n** stamp
der **Briefträger, -** mailman
der **Briefumschlag, ⸗e** envelope
bringen, brachte, gebracht, er bringt to bring
das **Brot, -e** bread
die **Brücke, -n** bridge
der **Bruder, ⸗** brother
das **Buch, ⸗er** book
der **Buchdruck** printing, typography
die **Buchdruckerkunst** art of printing
Buckle: Engl. historian, 1821–1862
bunt *adj.* gay-colored
der **Bürger, -** citizen
der **Bürgermeister, -** mayor

C

Caesar, Julius: Roman statesman and writer, 100–44 B.C.
der **Charakter, Charaktäre** character
die **Chemie** chemistry
chinesisch *adj.* of China
Confuzius: Chinese philosopher, 551–479 B.C.

D

da *adv.* there; *conj.* as, since, because
dabei *adv.* near by; at the same time, in doing so

das **Dach,** ⁼er roof
dafür *adv.* for it
dagegen *adv.* on the contrary; **dagegen sein** to be against it
damit *adv.* therewith, with it, with that; *conj.* so that, in order to
danach after that, according to that
danken to thank *with dat. of pers.;* **danke!** thanks!
dann *adv.* then, at that time
daraus out of (that, which); **sich nichts daraus machen** not mind it
darüber = **drüber** about that, concerning that
darum = **drum** therefore
darunter = **drunter** under that, among them
das *def. art.* the; *pron.* which, that
daß *conj.* that, so that
dauern to last, continue; **dauernd** *adv.* always, lasting
davon *adv.* of it; away; off
dazu *adv.* for it; at it, (that, them); for that purpose
dein *poss. pron.* your
denken, dachte, gedacht, er denkt to think; **denken an** to think of, remember
der **Denker,** - thinker
denn *conj.* for, because
der *def. art.* he; *pron.* he who
dessen *rel. pron.* whose
deutlich *adj.* distinct, clear
deutsch *adj.* German; **auf deutsch** in German
dichten to write poetry; **der Dichter,** - poet, writer
die **Dichtung, -en** poetry, fiction
dick *adj.* thick; stout, plump
der **Dieb, -e** thief
der **Diebstahl,** ⁼e theft, robbery
diejenigen *pron.* those
dienen to serve; **der Diener,** - servant; **der Dienst -e** service
dieser, diese, dieses (dies) *dem. adj. and pron.* this, that, this one
diesseits *prep. gen.* on this side of
das **Ding, -e** *or* -er thing, object, matter
dir *pers. pron.* you, to you; *dat. of* **du**
direkt *adj.* direct
dirigieren to direct, conduct; **der**

Direktor, Direktoren director, conductor
doch *adv.* but, yet, after all, surely, anyway; indeed, please
der **Doktor, Doktoren** physician
das **Dorf,** ⁼er village
dort *adv.* there
draußen *adv.* outside, out-of-doors
dreierlei *adj.* three kinds
drinnen *adv.* inside
drucken to print
duften to scent; **der Duft,** ⁼e fragrance
dulden to suffer; tolerate, put up with
dumm *adj.* stupid, foolish
dumpf *adj.* gloomy, dull
dunkel *adj.* dark; **die Dunkelheit** darkness
durch *prep. acc.* through; by means of
durchaus *adv.* quite, by all means
durch-fallen* to fail (as in an examination)
durch-machen to go through, experience, suffer
dürfen, durfte, gedurft, er darf *mod. aux.* to be allowed, may; **darf ich?** may I? **ich darf nicht** I am not allowed to
düster *adj.* dark, dismal

E

eben *adv.* just, just now
ebenso *adv.* just so; **ebenso gut** just as good; **ebenso gern** just as soon
die **Ecke, -n** corner
edel *adj.* **edler, am edelsten** noble; precious, excellent
ehe *conj.* before
ehren to honor
ehrlich *adj.* honest, honorable
eigen *adj.* own; particular
eigenartig *adj.* strange, peculiar
das **Eigentum** property
der **Eigentümer,** - owner
eigentümlich original, characteristic
ein, eine, ein *indef. art.* a, an; *num. adj.* one; *pron.* **einer, eine, ein(e)s; einer** one, somebody
ein-berufen* to call in

sich **ein-bilden** to imagine, believe
ein-brechen* to break in
eindringlich *adj.* impressive, urgent
einige *indef. pron.* some, several
ein-kaufen to buy, purchase
ein-laden, lud ein, eingeladen, er lädt ein to invite; **die Einladung, -en** invitation
einmal once; **noch einmal** once more
ein-prägen to impress
ein-reichen to hand in, present
einsam *adj.* lonely, solitary
ein-sehen* to realize
ein-sprechen: (einem etwas) to instill; persuade, influence
einst: wie einst as formerly; once upon a time
die **Eintracht** harmony
ein-tragen* to enter (in a book)
ein-weihen to initiate, inaugurate, dedicate
ein-ziehen* to move in
einzig *adj.* only, sole, single
das **Elend** misery
die **Eltern,** *pl.* parents
das **Ende, -s, -n** end; **zu Ende bringen** to finish
endlich *adj.* final; *adv.* finally, at last
endlos *adj.* endless, continuously
eng *adj.* narrow; tight
der **Enkel, -** grandson, grandchild
entdecken to discover
die **Entfernung, -en** distance
entgegen *adv.* towards; **entgegen eilen** to hurry to meet
entgegnen to reply, answer
entkommen* to get away, escape
entlassen* to dismiss, discharge
entleihen* to borrow
sich **entscheiden*** to decide; **die Entscheidung, -en** decision
der **Entschluß, ⁼e** resolution
sich **entschuldigen** to excuse; apologize
enttäuschen to disappoint
entweder - oder *conj.* either - or
die **Epoche, -n** era, time
die **Erde, -n** earth; ground; **auf Erden** on earth
der **Erebus:** Gr. mythol. The gloomy space through which souls passed to Hades

erfahren* to hear, learn; **die Erfahrung, -en** experience
erfinden* to invent; **die Erfindung, -en** invention
der **Erfolg, -e** success, result
erfolgreich *adj.* successful
erforschen to explore; discover
erfüllen to fulfill, realize, end; **in Erfüllung gehen** to come true
ergreifen, ergriff, ergriffen, er ergreift to seize
erhalten* to get, receive; maintain
erkranken to get sick
sich **erkundigen** to inquire
erlauben to permit; **sich erlauben** to take the liberty; **die Erlaubnis, -se** permission
erleben to experience; **das Erlebnis, -se** experience, adventure
ernennen to appoint
ernst *adj.* earnest, serious
ernten to harvest; **die Ernte, -n** harvest, crop
eröffnen to open; inaugurate
ersehen* to see, notice, learn
erst *adj.* first; only; *adv.* at first, first of all; **zum erstenmal** for the first time
erstaunt *adj.* astonished, surprised
erwarten to expect; **die Erwartung** expectation
erwerben, erwarb, erworben, er erwirbt to obtain, acquire
erzählen to tell, relate; **die Erzählung, -en** narration; **erzähle!** tell me!
erziehen* to educate, train; **die Erziehung** education
es *pron.* it; **es gibt** there is, there are *with acc.*
Eschenbach, Ebner Marie: Austrian novelist, 1830-1916
essen, aß, gegessen, er ißt to eat; **das Essen** food, meal
etwas *indef. pron.* some, something, somewhat; **etwas länger** a little longer; **etwas anders** something else
euch *acc. and dat. of pron.* **ihr** you, to you
euer *gen. pl. of pron.* **du;** *poss. adj.* your, your own

das **Europa** Europe; **europäisch** *adj.* European

ewig *adj.* everlasting; eternal

das **Examen, Examina** examination

exportieren to export

F

die **Fabrik, -en** factory

fabrizieren to manufacture

fähig sein to be able

fahren, fuhr, ist gefahren, er fährt to ride, drive, travel, go

fallen, fiel, ist gefallen, er fällt to fall

die **Familie, -n** family

fangen, fing, gefangen, er fängt to catch, seize, capture

fast *adv.* almost, nearly

faul *adj.* lazy

fehlen to miss, make a mistake; be absent (in school)

der **Fehler, -** error, mistake

fehlerfrei *adj.* without fault, mistake

der **Feind, -e** enemy

das **Feld, -er** field

der **Fels = der Felsen, -en** rock, stone, cliff

das **Fenster, -** window

die **Ferien,** *pl.* vacation

fertig *adj. and adv.* finished, ready; **fertig machen** to finish; **sich fertig machen** to get ready; **fertig bringen** to finish

fest *adj.* firm; determined

das **Fest, -e** festival

fest-stellen to confirm, find out; identify (o. p.)

das **Feuer, -** fire; **um Feuer bitten** to ask for a light

finden, fand, gefunden, er findet to find

finster *adj.* dark; gloomy

fleißig *adj.* diligent, industrious; **der Fleiß** diligence

fliegen, flog, ist geflogen, er fliegt to fly

fliehen, floh, ist geflohen, er flieht to flee, escape

fließen, floß, ist geflossen, es fließt to flow

der **Flügel, -** wing

der **Flughafen, ≔** airport

das **Flugzeug, -e** airplane

der **Fluß, Flusses, Flüsse** river

folgen, ist gefolgt to follow; obey *with dat.*

forschen to search, investigate

fort *adv.* gone, off, away; **ich muß fort** I have to go

der **Fortschritt, -e** progress, advancement

fort-setzen to continue; **die Fortsetzung, -en** continuation

die **Frage, -n** question; **eine Frage stellen** to ask a question

fragen to ask; **fragen nach** to ask about; **fragend** questioning

Franklin, Benjamin: Amer. statesman and scientist, 1706–1790

(das) **Frankreich** France

französisch *adj.* French, of France

die **Frau, -en** woman, wife, Mrs.

das **Fräulein, -** young girl, Miss

frei *adj.* free, independent

die **Freiheit, -en** freedom, liberty

freiwillig *adj.* voluntary

fremd *adj.* foreign, strange; **der Fremde, -n** stranger, foreigner

die **Freude, -n** joy, pleasure

freudig *adj. and adv.* happily, joyful

sich freuen to be glad, be happy; **sich freuen auf** to look forward to; **es freut mich** I am glad, I am delighted

der **Freund, -e** friend; **die Freundin, -nen** (girl) friend

freundlich *adj.* friendly, kind; **aufs freundlichste** in a most friendly way

die **Freundschaft, -en** friendship

Freytag, Gustav: Germ. novelist and critic, 1816–1895

der **Friede, -ns, -n** peace

frieren to freeze

frisch *adj.* fresh; clean; cool

froh *adj. and adv.* happy, glad

fromm, frömmer, am frömmsten *adj.* pious, devout

die **Frucht, ≔e** fruit, crop

früh *adj.* early; soon; **heute früh** this morning

früher *adv.* formerly, earlier, sooner

der **Frühling, -e** spring
das **Frühstück, -e** breakfast
fühlen to feel; **sich fühlen** to feel
führen to lead, guide; **der Führer, -** leader
die **Fülle** abundance
die **Füllfeder, -n** fountain pen
der **Funke, -ns, -n** spark, flash
für *prep. acc.* for, for the sake of, on behalf of, instead of; **was für ein?** what kind of
sich **fürchten** to be afraid *with dat.;* die **Furcht** fear, fright
der **Fuß, Fußes, Füße** foot; **zu Fuß gehen** to walk, go on foot
der **Fußball, ⸗e** football
der **Fußboden, ⸗** floor

G

die **Galerie, -n** gallery
ganz *adj.* all, whole; *adv.* quite; **im ganzen** on the whole, generally
der **Garten, ⸗** garden
der **Gast, ⸗e** guest
das **Gasthaus, ⸗er** inn
geächtet *p. p.* outlawed
das **Gebäude, -** building
geben, gab, gegeben, er gibt to give, present; **es gibt, es gab** there is, there are
gebieten, gebot, geboten, er gebietet to order, rule
das **Gebirge, -** mountain range
geboren *p. p.* born; **die Geburt, -en** birth; **von Geburt** by birth
gebrauchen to use, make use of
der **Geburtstag, -e** birthday
das **Gedächtnis** memory
der **Gedächtniskram** mere matter of memory, mere cramming
das **Gedicht, -e** poem
die **Geduld** patience
geehrt *p. p.* honored, respected
der **Gefährte, -n, -n** companion
gefallen, gefiel, gefallen, er gefällt to please; **es gefällt mir** I like it; **sich gefallen lassen** to put up with; **der Soldat ist gefallen** died in battle
gefangen *p. p.* caught, captured;

gefangen setzen to imprison; **der Gefangene, -n, -n** prisoner
gegen *prep. acc.* against, contrary to; towards
die **Gegend, -en** region, district
das **Gegenteil, -e** opposite; **im Gegenteil** on the contrary
der **Gegner, -** opponent
das **Geheimnis, -ses, -se** secret
gehen, ging, ist gegangen, er geht to go, walk; **wie gehts? Danke, es geht mir gut** How are you? I am all right (fine)
gehorchen to obey *with dat.*
gehören to belong, be owned by *with dat.*
der **Geizhals, ⸗e** miser
das **Geld, -er** money; **bares Geld** cash
gelingen, gelang, ist gelungen, es gelingt to succeed *with dat.*
das **Gemälde, -** painting
das **Gemüt** heart, emotion, feeling
genial ingenious
genug *adv.* enough, sufficient
gerade = grade *adv.* just, now; *adj.* straight
gerecht *adj.* just, fair; **die Gerechtigkeit** justice, fairness
das **Gericht, -e** court of justice
gerichtlich *adj.* legally, judicially
gering *adj.* small; unimportant
gern *adv.* **lieber, am liebsten** gladly, with pleasure; **gern haben** to like
der **Gesang, ⸗e** singing, melody
das **Geschäft, -e** business; office
der **Geschäftsmann, Geschäftsleute** businessman
geschehen, geschah, ist geschehen, es geschieht to happen
das **Geschenk, -e** present
die **Geschichte, -n** story, history
der **Geschmack** taste
die **Geschwister,** *pl.* sisters and brothers
der **Geselle, -n, -n** companion, fellow
das **Gesetz, -e** law, regulation
das **Gesicht, -er** face
gestalten to form, turn out; **die Gestalt, -en** figure, form
das **Gestein, -e** stone, rock
gestern *adv.* yesterday; **gestern abend** last night

gestrandet *p. p.* stranded, shipwrecked

gesund *adj.* well, in good health; die **Gesundheit** health

die **Gewalt, -en** power, force; control

gewandt *adj.* clever, skillful

gewinnen, gewann, gewonnen, er gewinnt to win, earn; produce

gewiß *adv.* certainly, for sure; **gewisse Dinge** certain things, matters

gewissenhaft *adj.* conscientious

sich **gewöhnen** to accustom o. s., get used to *with acc.*

gewöhnlich *adv.* usually

gießen, goß, gegossen, er gießt to pour

glänzen to glitter, shine

das **Glas, -es, =er** glass

der **Glaube, -ns, -n** belief, faith

glauben to believe *with dat. of pers.*

gleich *adv.* at once, right away; *adj.* same, alike

die **Glocke, -n** bell

das **Glück** fortune, good luck

glücken to succeed, turn out well

glücklich *adj.* happy; **glückliche Reise!** safe journey! have a pleasant trip!

glücklicherweise *adv.* fortunately

Goethe, Johann Wolfgang: Germ. poet and dramatist, 1749–1832

Gott God; **Gott bewahre!** God forbid!

graben, grub, gegraben, er gräbt to dig; der **Graben, =** ditch

das **Gras, -es, =er** grass

grau *adj.* gray

greifen, griff, gegriffen, er greift to grasp, catch, seize

der **Grieche, -n, -n** Greek

Grillparzer, Franz: Austrian dramatist, 1791–1872

groß, größer, am größten *adj.* large, tall; important

großartig *adj.* grand, magnificent

die **Großeltern,** *pl.* grandparents

der **Grundsatz, =e** principle; rule of conduct

grüßen to greet; **grüßen lassen** to send one's regards

gut, besser, am besten good, kind, friendly

das **Gute** the good, the desirable, the beneficial

Gutenberg, Johann: Germ. inventor of printing from movable type

H

das **Haar, -e** hair

haben, hatte, gehabt, er hat to have

Haeckel, Ernst: Germ. biologist and philosopher, 1834–1919

der **Hafen, =** harbor

halb *adj.* half; *adv.* **halb zwei** half past one

halten, hielt, gehalten, er hält to hold; keep

die **Hand, =e** hand

der **Handel** trade, commerce, business

handeln to act; deal, trade

die **Handelsgesellschaft, -en** trading company

die **Handschrift, -en** penmanship

das **Handwerkszeug,** *pl.* tools

hängen, hing, gehangen, es hängt to hang; attach

Hartmann, Eduard v.: Germ. philosopher, 1842–1906

hassen to hate; der **Haß** hate, hatred

das **Haus, =er** house, home; **nach Hause** home; **zu Hause** at home

die **Hautfarbe, -n** color of the skin

heftig *adj.* violent

Heidelberg: city in West Germany

die **Heimat, -en** home-town, homeland

heiraten to marry, get married

heiß *adj.* hot, burning

heißen, hieß, geheißen, er heißt to be called; **wie heißen Sie?** what is your name?

der **Held, -en, -en** hero

helfen, half, geholfen, er hilft to help

herab *adv.* down; **herabsetzen** to lower; reduce

herauf *adv.* up, upwards

herbei-wünschen to wish for, bring about

der **Herbst, -e** autumn; **im kommenden Herbst** next fall

die **Herde, -n** herd, flock

Herder, Johann Gottfried: Germ. philosopher and writer

herein *adv. and sep. pref.* in, into

Hermann und Dorothea: epic poem by Goethe

der **Herr, -n, -en** master; ruler; Mr.

herrlich *adj.* wonderful, splendid

herum *adv. and sep. pref.* around; **um herum** all the way around

das **Herz, -ens, -en** heart

herzlich *adj. and adv.* cordially, sincerely

heute *adv.* today; **heute morgen** this morning; **heute abend** tonight

hier *adv.* here; **von hier aus** from this place

hierher *adv.* to this place

die **Hilfe, -n** help, assistance

der **Himmel, -** sky; heaven; **am Himmel** in the sky

hinab *adv.* down, downwards

hinauf *adv.* up, upwards

hindurch *adv.* through, throughout

hinein *adv.* in, into

hin-geben* to give up, sacrifice

hinten *adv.* in back

hinter *prep. dat. or acc.* behind

hinterlassen* to leave behind; bequeath

der **Hirt, -en, -en** shepherd

die **Hitze** heat

hoch, *adj.* **höher, am höchsten** high; **höchst** *adv.* very, highly

hochgeachtet *adj.* highly esteemed, respected

hoffen to hope (for), expect; **die Hoffnung, -en** hope

holen to fetch, get

Horaz: Horace, Quintus: Roman poet and satirist, 65–8 B.C.

hören to hear

der **Hörsaal, Hörsäle** lecture room

Humboldt, Alexander v.: Germ. naturalist and statesman, 1769–1859

der **Hund, -e** dog

hungrig *adj.* hungry

der **Hut, ⸗e** hat

hüten to guard, watch

I

das **Ideal, -e** ideal

die **Idee, Ide-en** idea; thought

ihnen *pers. pron.* them

ihr *pers. pron.* you

ihr, ihre, ihr *poss. adj.* her, its, their; **Ihr, Ihre, Ihr** your

Ihring, Rudolf: Germ. jurist and historian, 1818–1892

immer *adv.* always, ever; **immer wieder** again and again; **immer nur** always

importieren to import

in *prep. dat. or acc.* in, into

innerhalb *prep. gen.* within, inside of

der **Inspektor, -s, -en** inspector

das **Interesse, -n** interest

interessieren to interest; **sich interessieren** to take an interest (in)

sich irren to be mistaken

der **Irrtum, ⸗er** error, mistake; **im Irrtum sein** to be mistaken

(das) **Italien** Italy

J

ja yes, indeed, to be sure

das **Jahr, -e** year; **vor einem Jahr** a year ago; **im nächsten Jahr** next year; **sieben Jahre lang** for seven years; **seit langen Jahren** for many years

die **Jahreszeit, -en** season

das **Jahrhundert, -e** century

je *adv.* ever, always

jedenfalls *adv.* in any case; however

jeder, jede, jedes *pron.* each, everyone

jemand *indef. pron.* somebody

jener, jene, jenes *pron.* that, that one, the former

jenseits *prep. gen.* on the other side of

jetzt *adv.* now

die **Jugend, -** youth, young people

jung, jünger, am jüngsten *adj.* young

der **Junge, -n, -n** boy, lad, youth

der **Jüngling, -e** young man

K

der **Kaffee** coffee

kalt, kälter, am kältesten *adj.* cold

kämmen to comb

kämpfen to fight

der **Kandidat, -en, -en** candidate
Kant, Immanuel: German philosopher, 1724–1804
der **Kantor, -s, -en** cantor; singer, leader of a church choir
die **Karte, -n** card, (admission) ticket
kaufen to buy
die **Kaufsumme, -n** purchase money
kaum *adv.* hardly, scarcely
kein, keine, kein *adj. and pron.* no, no one, not any; **keiner** nobody, not one
keineswegs *adv.* by no means
Keller, Gottfried: Swiss novelist
kennen, kannte, gekannt, er kennt to know, be acquainted with
die **Kenntnis, -se** knowledge
die **Kette, -n** chain; necklace
das **Kind, er** child
die **Kirche, -n** church
klagen to complain
der **Klang, ⁼e** timbre, music
klar *adj.* clear, plain, bright
das **Klassenzimmer, -** classroom
das **Kleid, -er** dress
sich **kleiden** to dress
klein *adj.* little, small
klingen, klang, geklungen, es klingt to sound; ring
klopfen to knock
klug, klüger, am klügsten *adj.* intelligent, clever; **die Klugheit** intelligence, good sense
der **Knabe, -n, -n** boy
Köln: city of Cologne
kommen, kam, ist gekommen, er kam to come, arrive; **das Kommen** the arrival; **kommen lassen** to send for
der **König, -e** king; **die Königin, -nen** queen
können, konnte, gekonnt, er kann *mod. aux.* can, be able to; know (how to)
die **Kontrolle, -n** control
das **Konzert, -e** concert
das **Korn, ⁼er** corn; grain
korrigieren to correct
kosten to cost; to require
der **Kram** trash; odds and ends
krank *adj.* sick; **die Krankheit, -en** sickness

sich **kränken** to grieve; offend; **das kränkt** that hurts
die **Kreuzung, -en** crossing (street)
der **Krieg, -e** war
die **Küche, -n** kitchen
der **Kuchen, -** cake
kühl *adj.* cool
kultivieren to cultivate
die **Kultur, -en** culture; civilization
sich **kümmern** to care, be concerned; **sich kümmern um** to trouble about
der **Künstler, -** artist; **die Künstlerin, -nen** woman artist
kurz, kürzer, am kürzesten *adj.* short; brief; **kurz vorher** short time before
die **Küste, -n** coast, shore

L

lächeln to smile
lachen to laugh
die **Lampe, -n** lamp
das **Land, ⁼er** land, soil; country; **auf dem Lande** in the country; **aufs Land** to the country
landen to land, get ashore
lang, länger, am längsten *adj. and adv.* long; **lange** for a long time; **noch lange** for a long time; **lange nicht** not for a long time
langsam *adj. and adv.* slow, slowly
langweilig *adj.* boring, dull
der **Lärm** noise
lassen, ließ, gelassen, er läßt to allow, permit; order; **holen lassen** to send for; **warten lassen** to keep waiting
lateinisch *adj.* Latin; **das Latein** Latin
laufen, lief, ist gelaufen, er läuft to run; to flow
laut *adj.* loud, noisy
läuten to ring (a bell)
leben to live, stay; to dwell; **das Leben** life, existence
lehren to teach, instruct; **der Lehrer, -** teacher, instructor
leicht *adj. and adv.* light, easy; probably
leichtsinnig *adj.* thoughtless

leiden, litt, gelitten, er leidet to suffer; **das Leid, -en** grief, sorrow; **es tut mir leid** I am sorry; „**Die Leiden des jungen Werthers**": *"The Sorrows of Young Werther"*, an epistolary novel by Wolfgang Goethe

leihen, lieh, geliehen, er leiht to lend

leise *adj. and adv.* low, soft

Leisewitz, Johann: German dramatist, 1752–1806

lernen to learn, study

lesen, las, gelesen, er liest to read

Lessing, Gotthold: German dramatist and critic, 1729–1781

letzt *adj.* last; latest; final

leugnen to deny

die **Leute,** *pl.* people

das **Licht, -er** light; (*pl.* **-e**) candle

lieben to love, to be in love; die **Liebe** love, affection; **lieb haben** to love

lieber (*comparative of* **gern**) rather

lieblich *adj.* lovely, sweet, delightful

liebst (*superlative of* **gern**) dearest, most beloved

das **Lied, -er** song

liegen, lag, gelegen, er liegt to lie, be situated; **liegen lassen** to let lie; leave; **was liegt darin?** what is there about it?

links *adv.* on (to) the left

die **List, -en** cunning, intrigue

die **Literatur, -en** literature

loben to praise

der **Lohn, ⸗e** wage, reward

löschen to extinguish

lösen to loosen, untie; solve; answer

der **Löwe, -n, -n** lion

die **Luft, ⸗e** air

lügen, log, gelogen, er lügt to tell a lie

M

machen to make, do; **machen lassen** to have made

die **Macht, ⸗e** power, might

mächtig *adj.* powerful, strong

das **Mädchen, -** girl

Magna Charta: the Great Charter of liberties, to which English barons forced King John's assent, June 1215

der **Mai** month of May

malen to paint; der **Maler, -** painter

man *indef. pron.* one, people

mancher, manche, manches some, many a; *pl.* many

manchmal *adv.* sometimes

der **Mann, ⸗er** man, husband

der **Mantel, ⸗** overcoat

das **Märchen, -** fairy tale

Mark Aurel: Roman Emperor and philosopher, 121–180 A.D.

der **Markt, ⸗e** market; market place

marschieren to march

das **Material, -s, -ien** material

die **Mauer, -n** wall

die **Maus, ⸗e** mouse

die **Medizin, -en** medicine

das **Meer, -e** sea, ocean

mehr *adv.* more; **mehr als** more than; **nicht mehr** no longer

mehrere *adj. pl.* several

mehrfach *adj. and adv.* repeatedly

mein *poss. pron.* my

meinen to mean, believe, say; die **Meinung, -en** opinion

meist *adj. and adv.* most, mostly; **meistens** mostly

der **Meister, -** master; boss

der **Mensch, -en, -en** human being, man; *pl.* people

das **Menschengeschlecht, -er** human race

menschlich *adj.* human

merken to notice, observe; **sich merken** to remember

das **Messer, -** knife

mich *acc. of pron.* **ich** me

mieten to rent

die **Milch** milk

mindest *adj.* least, smallest; **mindestens** *adv.* at least

mir *dat. of pron.* **ich** me, to me

mischen to mix; die **Mischung, -en** mixture, compound

der **Missionar, -e** missionary

mit *prep. dat.* with, by, at

mit-bringen* to bring along

der **Mitbürger, -** fellow citizen

mit-gehen* to go along

das **Mitleid** pity, compassion

der **Mitmensch, -en** fellow-man; one's neighbor

mit-nehmen* to take along

der **Mittag, -e** noon; **zu Mittag essen** to eat dinner

mit-teilen to tell, inform, notify

das **Mittel, -** means; remedy

die **Mitternacht** midnight; **mitternachts** *adv.* at midnight

mögen, mochte, gemocht, er mag *mod. aux.* may, to like, to care to; **ich mag nicht** I don't like to

der **Monat, -e** month

der **Mond, -e** moon

der **Morgen, -** morning; **morgen** *adv.* tomorrow; **heute morgen** this morning; **morgen früh** tomorrow morning; **morgen abend** tomorrow night

der **Motor, -en** motor

müde *adj.* tired, weary

(das) **München:** city of Munich

der **Mund, -e,** or **ⁿer** mouth

müssen, mußte, gemußt, er muß *mod. aux.* must, have to

der **Mut** courage; **mutig** *adj.* brave

die **Mutter, ⁼** mother

N

nach *prep. dat.* after, to, towards; **nach Hause** home

das **Nachahmen** imitation

der **Nachbar, -s, -n** neighbor

nachdem *adv.* afterwards; *conj.* after

das **Nachdenken** thinking, reflection

nachmittags *adv.* in the afternoon

die **Nachricht, -en** news; notice

nächst *adj. and adv.* nearest, shortest

die **Nacht, ⁼e** night; **nachts** *adv.* at night

nächtlich *adj.* nightly

der **Nagel, ⁼** nail

nah, näher, am nächsten *adj.* near by, close by

der **Name, -ns, -n** name; **im Namen** in the name of, under the pretext of

der **Narr, -en, -en; die Närrin, -nen** fool

die **Natur** nature

die **Naturwissenschaft, -en** natural science

Neapel: city of Naples

der **Nebel, -** fog, mist

neben *prep. dat. or acc.* next to, besides

nehmen, nahm, genommen, er nimmt to take; to seize

nennen, nannte, genannt, er nennt to call, name

neu *adj.* new, recent

nicht *adv.* not; **gar nicht** not at all; **noch nicht** not yet; **nicht mehr** no longer; **nicht wahr?** isn't it so? **nicht einmal** not once, not even

nichts *adv.* nothing; **gar nichts** nothing at all; **nichts mehr** nothing; **ein Nichts** a mere nothing

das **Nickel** nickel (metal)

nie *adv.* never

niemals *adv.* never

niemand *indef. pron.* nobody

nirgend *pron.* nowhere

noch *adv.* still, yet; **noch immer** still; **noch nicht** not yet; **noch nie** never; **noch gestern** as late as yesterday; **noch einmal** once more

der **Norden** North

die **Not, ⁼e** need, want; **Not leiden** to be in want, in distress

nötig *adj.* necessary

die **Novelle, -n** (short) story

die **Nummer, -n** number

nur *adv.* only

nützen to be of use; **nützlich** *adj.* useful; **nichts nützen** useless

O

ob *conj.* whether, if; **als ob** as if

oben *adv.* above, at the top; **dort oben** up there; **nach oben** upwards

obgleich *conj.* although

das **Obst, ** *pl.* fruit

oder, *conj.* or

der **Ofen, ⁼** stove; fireside

offen *adj.* open

öffnen to open

oft *adv.* often; **öfter** more often, more frequent

ohne *prep. acc.* without

das **Ohr, -en** ear
der **Onkel, -** uncle
opfern to sacrifice
die **Ordnung** order; arrangement
(das) **Österreich** Austria

P

paar: ein paar a few, some
das **Paar, -e** pair; couple
das **Paket, -e** package, parcel, bundle
der **Papierkorb, ⸗e** wastepaper basket
der **Park, -e** park
persönlich *adj.* personal
der **Pfarrer, -** clergyman, minister
pflanzen to plant; **die Pflanze, -n** plant
die **Pflicht, -en** duty
pflücken to pick, gather
pflügen to plough
der **Plan, ⸗e** plan, project
planen to plan, project
der **Planet, -en, -en** planet
der **Platz, ⸗e** place, (village) square
plötzlich *adv.* suddenly
der **Polizist, -en** policeman
die **Post = das Postamt, ⸗er** post office
der **Präsident, -en, -en** president; chairman
der **Preis, -e** price, cost
(das) **Preußen** Prussia
der **Professor, -s, -en** professor
das **Projekt, -e** project
der **Prophet, -en, -en** prophet
pünktlich *adj. and adv.* punctual

R

die **Ränke** *pl.* intrigues
der **Rat, Ratschläge** advice; **um Rat fragen** to ask for advice
raten, riet, geraten, er rät to advise; to guess
das **Rathaus, ⸗er** city hall
das **Rätsel, -** riddle, puzzle
die **Ratte, -n** rat
rauchen to smoke
rechnen to count
die **Rechnung, -en** account, bill

das **Recht, -e** right; law
recht *adj. and adv.* right, correct, just; *adv.* very, really, quite; **recht haben** to be right; **recht arm** quite poor; **die rechte Hand** right hand
rechts *adv.* on (to) the right
reden to speak, talk; **die Rede, -n** speech
der **Redner, -** speaker, lecturer
die **Regel, -n** rule; regulation
regelmäßig *adj.* regular, always
der **Regen, -** rain, shower; **starker Regen** heavy rain
sich **regen** to move, stir; **die Regung, -en** impulse, motivation
der **Regent, -en, -en** ruler
regieren to rule, govern; **die Regierung, -en** government
regnen to rain
reich *adj.* rich, plentiful
das **Reich, -e** realm, empire
reichen to reach, extend
reichlich *adj.* abundantly
der **Reichtum, ⸗er** riches, wealth
reif *adj.* ripe
die **Reihe, -n** row, line, number
rein *adj.* pure, clean, clear
sich **reinigen** to clear o. s.; to clean
reisen, ist gereist to go, travel; **die Reise, -n** trip, journey; **glückliche Reise!** farewell! pleasant trip!
reißen, riß, gerissen, er reißt to tear
reiten, ritt, ist geritten, er reitet to ride (on horseback)
rennen, rannte, ist gerannt, er rennt to run
restlos *adj.* entirely, to the end
retten to save, rescue
der **Rhein:** river Rhine
der **Richter, -** judge
richtig *adj.* correct, right; **das Richtige** the correct, the true
der **Ring, -e** ring
Rochefort, Victor Henri, French writer and statesman, 1881–1913
die **Rolle, -n** rôle, part (in theater)
die **Rose, -n** rose
rot *adj.* red
rufen, rief, gerufen, er ruft to call; **rufen lassen** to send for

ruhen to rest; die Ruhe, -n rest; silence; peace
ruhig *adj.* quiet, peaceful
der Ruhm fame, glory
rühren to move, stir
russisch *adj.* Russian; das Rußland Russia

S

der Saal, Säle hall
die Sache, -n thing, matter, affair
säen to sow
sagen to say, tell
die Salpetersäure nitric acid
der Same, -ns, -n seed
sammeln to collect; die Sammlung, -en collection
der Samstag = der Sonnabend, -e Saturday
der Satz, ⸗e sentence
der Sauerstoff oxygen
die Säure, -n acid
schaden to harm, injure; der Schaden, ⸗ damage
das Schauspiel, -e play, drama
der Schauspieler, - actor; die Schauspielerin, -nen actress
die Scheibe, -n pane of glass
der Schein, -e shine, light; certificate; ticket
scheinen, schien, geschienen, es scheint to shine; seem, appear
scheitern to shipwreck, run aground
schenken to give, present
schicken to send
das Schicksal, -e fate
die Schicksalsschläge *pl.* blows of fate
schießen, schoß, geschossen, er schießt to shoot
das Schiff, -e ship, steamer
der Schiffer, - seaman, sailor; skipper
Schiller, Friedrich: German poet and dramatist, 1759–1805
die Schlacht, -en battle
schlafen, schlief, geschlafen, er schläft to sleep
schlagen, schlug, geschlagen, er schlägt to strike
schlank *adj.* slender, tall

schlecht *adj.* bad, poor; wicked; am schlechtesten the worst
schließen, schloß, geschlossen, er schließt to close, lock; to finish, end; Frieden schließen to make peace
das Schloß, Schlosses, Schlösser castle
der Schluß, Schlusses, Schlüsse end, conclusion
der Schlüssel, - key
der Schmerz, -es, -en pain
der Schnee snow
schneiden, schnitt, geschnitten, er schneidet to cut; der Schneider - tailor
schneien to snow
schnell *adj.* quick, fast
schon *adv.* already, by this time
schön *adj.* beautiful, nice
Schopenhauer, Arthur: German philosopher, 1788–1860
(das) Schottland Scotland
der Schrecken, -s, - fright, terror; in Schrecken setzen to terrify, frighten
schreiben, schrieb, geschrieben, er schreibt to write
der Schreibtisch, -e desk, writing table
der Schuh, -e shoe
die Schularbeit, -en homework
die Schuld, -en debt; blame, fault
die Schule, -n school; zur Schule to school
der Schüler, - pupil; die Schülerin, -nen girl pupil
das Schulkind, -er pupil
das Schulgeld, -er tuition
Schumann, Robert: German composer, 1810–1856
schützen to protect, guard; der Schutz protection, shelter
schwach, schwächer, am schwächsten *adj.* weak, frail; small; poor; die Schwäche weakness
schwarz, schwärzer, am schwärzesten black; dark
die Schweiz Switzerland
schwer *adj.* heavy, difficult; es fällt mir schwer I find it difficult; schwer verwundet badly (seriously) wounded

die **Schwester, -n** sister
schwimmen, schwamm, geschwom-men, er schwimmt to swim
der **See, Se-es, Se-en** lake
die **See, Se-en** ocean; **an der See** by the seaside
die **Seele, -n** soul; heart
segnen to bless; **der Segen, -** blessing
sehen, sah, gesehen, er sieht to see, look
sich **sehnen** to long for
sehr *adv.* very; **sehr gut** very well; **sehr gern** gladly; **sehr wenig** very little
sein, war, ist gewesen, er ist to be
sein *poss. adj.* his, hers, its
seinerzeit *adv.* in his time
seit *prep. dat. and conj.* since; **seit drei Tagen** for three days; **seitdem** since then
die **Seite, -n** page; side
selber *pron.:* **ich selber** I myself; itself
selbst *adv.* even; **von selbst** by itself; **in ihm selbst** within himself
selten *adj.* rare; scarce; *adv.* seldom
der **Senator, -s, -en** senator
senden, sandte, gesandt, er sendet to send, dispatch
Seneca, Lucius: Roman statesman and philosopher, 4 B.C.–65 A.D.
setzen to set, put; **sich setzen** to sit down; **setzen Sie sich!** please, sit down
sich *refl. pron.* himself, herself, itself, myself; -selves
sicher *adj.* secure, safe; *adv.* certainly
sie *pers. pron.* she, her; they; **Sie** you
das **Silber** silver
singen, sang, gesungen, er singt to sing
der **Sinn, -e** mind, intellect
sitzen, saß, gesessen, er sitzt to sit; **die Sitzung, -en** meeting
so *adv.* so, thus; *conj.* therefore
sobald *conj.* as soon as
sofort *adv.* at once, immediately
der **Sohn, ⸚e** son
solange *conj.* as long as
solcher, solche, solches, solch *pron.* such

der **Soldat, -en, -en** soldier
sollen *mod. aux.* shall, ought, should
der **Sommer, -** summer
sonderbar *adj.* strange, peculiar
sonst *adv.* otherwise; formerly; usually; **sonst etwas?** anything else? **sonst nichts?** nothing else? **sonst wie** in any other way
sorgen to care for; provide for; **die Sorge, -n** sorrow, trouble
sorgfältig *adj.* careful
(das) **Spanien** Spain; **spanisch** of Spain
sparsam *adj.* thrifty
spät *adj.* late; **später** later
spazieren gehen to take a walk
der **Spaziergang, ⸚e** (pleasure) walk; **einen Spaziergang machen** to take a walk
spielen to play; **das Spiel, -e** play, game
spitz *adj.* pointed; **die Spitze, -n** point, top
die **Sprache, -n** language, speech
sprechen, sprach, gesprochen, er spricht to speak, talk
springen, sprang, ist gesprungen, er springt to jump, leap
der **Staat, -en** state
der **Staatsmann, ⸚er** statesman, diplomat
die **Stadt, ⸚e** city
die **Stadtkasse, -n** city treasury
stark, stärker, am stärksten *adj.* strong; heavy (rain); **die Stärke** strength
stecken to stick, put (into)
stehen, stand, gestanden, er steht to stand; **wie steht es?** how are (things)? how about?
stehen bleiben* to stop
stehlen, stahl, gestohlen, er stiehlt to steal; rob
steigen, stieg, ist gestiegen, er steigt to climb, ascend
steil *adj.* steep
der **Stein, -e** stone
die **Stelle, -n** place, spot
stellen to put, place; **eine Frage stellen** to ask a question
die **Stellung, -en** position, job
sterben, starb, gestorben, er stirbt to die

der **Stern, -e** star
die **Steuer, -n** tax, assessment
der **Stickstoff** nitrogen
still *adj.* still, calm; silent; lonely
still stehen* to stop, stand still
die **Stimme, -n** voice; vote
stimmen to vote; to agree or disagree with
die **Stirn, -en** forehead, brow
stolz *adj.* proud
stören to disturb, interrupt
stranden to strand, be shipwrecked
die **Straße, -n** street; highway; **auf der Straße** in the street
streben to strive, struggle
streiten, stritt, gestritten, er streitet to quarrel, fight; **der Streit, -e** fight
der **Strom, ⸗e** stream, (large) river
das **Stück, -e** piece; play (theater)
der **Student, -en, -en** student
die **Studi-e, Studi-en** study
die **Studien,** *pl.* studies, pursuits; education
studieren to study
das **Studium** course of study
der **Stuhl, ⸗e** chair
die **Stunde, -n** hour; lesson
der **Sturm, ⸗e** storm
Stuttgart: name of a city
suchen to search, look for
der **Süden** South
die **Summe, -n** sum, amount
süß *adj.* sweet

T

der **Tag, -e** day, **am Tage** during the day; **eines Tages** one day; **den ganzen Tag** all day long; **drei Tage lang** for three days
die **Tageszeitung, -en** daily newspaper
täglich *adj. and adv.* daily
das **Tal, ⸗er** valley
die **Tanne, -n** fir tree
tanzen to dance; **der Tanz, ⸗e** dance; **der Tänzer, -** dancer
tapfer *adj.* brave
die **Tasche, -n** pocket; handbag
die **Tasse, -n** cup
die **Tat, -en** deed, action; **tätig sein** to be active; at work

die **Taube, -n** pigeon, dove
taugen to be good for, fit for
teilen to divide, share; **geteilt durch** divided by
telephonieren to telephone
telegraphieren to send a telegram
teuer *adj.* expensive
Thant, U: Secretary General, UN
das **Theater, -** theater; stage
Thibeaut, Jacques: French violinist, 1880–1953
tief *adj.* deep; low (voice)
das **Tier, -e** animal
der **Tierarzt, ⸗e** veterinarian
der **Tisch, -e** table
die **Tochter, ⸗** daughter
der **Tod** death
der **Todfeind, -e** deadly enemy
tödlich *adj.* fatal, deadly
tot *adj.* dead
der **Tourist, -en** tourist, traveler
trachten to strive, aspire
tragen, trug, getragen, er trägt to carry, bear, wear
die **Träne, -n** tear
trauen to trust
träumen to dream; **der Traum, ⸗e** dream
treffen, traf, getroffen, er trifft to meet
die **Treppe, -n** staircase, stairs
treten, trat, ist getreten, er tritt to step, walk; **ins Haus treten** to enter the house
treu *adj.* faithful, loyal
trinken, trank, getrunken, er trinkt to drink
trocken *adj.* dry; arid
trotz *prep. gen.* in spite of
tüchtig *adj.* able, efficient
die **Tücke, -n** malice, treachery
tun, tat, getan, er tut to do, act, work; **es tut mir leid** I am sorry; **es wird getan** will be done
die **Tür, -en** door

U

über *prep. da. or acc.* over, above, across, about
überhaupt *adv.* in general, at all, on the whole
übernehmen* to take over

überraschen to surprise
übersetzen to translate
überzeugen to convince
die Übung, -en exercise
das Ufer, - shore, bank (of a river)
die Uhr, -en clock, watch; **um zehn Uhr** at ten o'clock
um *prep. acc.* around, about, at, for; **umher** all around; **um sechs Uhr** at six o'clock
die Umgebung, -en environs, surrounding country
unaufhörlich *adj.* constant, continuous
unbeachtet *adj. and adv.* unnoticed
unbedeutend *adj.* insignificant
unbekannt *adj.* unknown, strange; a stranger to
unbeugsam *adj.* unbending; stubborn, firm
undeutlich *adj.* indistinct
unermeßlich *adj.* immense, immeasurable
unerwartet *adj. and adv.* unexpected, sudden
der Unfall, ⸗e accident
ungeduldig *adj.* impatient; **die Ungeduld** impatience
ungerecht *adj.* unjust, unfair
ungern *adv.* unwillingly
das Unglück, Unglücksfälle misfortune, disaster
das Unheil harm, trouble, disaster
unhöflich *adj.* impolite, rude
die Universität, -en university; **auf der Universität** at the university
unmöglich *adj.* impossible
das Unrecht wrong, injustice; **Unrecht haben** to be in the wrong
uns *acc. and dat. of* wir us, to us
unser *pron. and poss. adj.* ours; of us
unsere = unsrige *pron.* our, our people
unsicher *adj.* uncertain; insecure
unten *adv.* below
unter *prep. dat. or acc.* under, below; among
unter-gehen* to sink
unterhalten* to support, maintain
unterhandeln to negotiate
unterrichten to teach, instruct

unterscheiden to distinguish;
der Unterschied, -e difference
untersuchen to investigate
unterzeichnen to sign, ratify
unvergleichlich incomparable, matchless
unversehens *adv.* unexpectedly
unzuverlässig unreliable
der Ursprung origin; **ursprünglich** *adv.* originally

V

der Vater, ⸗ father
die Verabredung, -en agreement
verbannen to banish, exile
verbieten, verbot, verboten, er verbietet to forbid
das Verbrechen, - crime
verderben, verdarb, verdorben, er verdirbt to spoil
verdienen to earn; deserve
verehren to respect, venerate
die Vereinten Nationen *pl.* United Nations
verfolgen to follow, pursue
vergeben to forgive, pardon
vergebens *adv.* in vain
vergeblich *adj.* in vain, futile
vergessen, vergaß, vergessen, er vergißt to forget
das Vergnügen, - pleasure, enjoyment, amusement; **Vergnügen bereiten** to give pleasure; to take delight in
verheiraten to marry; **sich verheiraten** to get married
verkaufen to sell
verlassen, verließ, verlassen, er verläßt to leave; **sich verlassen auf** to depend upon
verletzen to hurt, injure
verlieren, verlor, verloren, er verliert to lose
der Verlust, -e loss
vermuten to suspect
vernichten to destroy
vernünftig *adj.* reasonable; logical; **die Vernunft** reason, judgment
verpassen to miss (train)
verraten, verriet, verraten, er verrät to betray; **der Verrat** treason

verreisen to go on a trip; to travel
versagen to deny
versammeln to assemble, gather; **um sich versammeln** to surround themselves (with)
verschieden *adj.* different
verschwenden to squander
verschwiegen *p. p.* discreet; **die Verschwiegenheit** silence, discretion
versprechen* to promise
der **Verstand** sense, intelligence; mind
verstecken to hide, conceal
verstehen* to understand; to know how
versuchen to try
der **Vertrag, ⸗e** agreement, treaty
vertrauen to trust; rely upon
vertreiben, vertrieb, vertrieben, er vertreibt to drive away; expel
verurteilen, to sentence
verwandeln to change
verwandt *adj.* related; **der Verwandte, -n** relative
verweigern to refuse
verzeihen, verzieh, verziehen, er verzeiht to pardon, forgive
viel *adv.* **mehr, am meisten** much; often; **viele** many; **wieviel?** how much? **wie viele?** how many? **viel gelesen** widely read
vielleicht *adv.* perhaps
der **Vogel, ⸗** bird
das **Volk, ⸗er** people, nation
das **Volkslied, -er** folk song
voll *adj.* full, filled
von *prep. dat.* from, of
vor *prep. dat. or acc.* before, in front of, from; **vor einem Jahr** a year ago
sich **vor-bereiten** to prepare
vor-lesen* to read aloud
die **Vorlesung, -en** lecture; **eine Vorlesung halten** to give a lecture
der **Vormittag, -e** forenoon; **am Vormittag** in the forenoon
vorn *adv.* in front
sich **vor-nehmen*** to intend (to do); **sich etwas vornehmen** to make up one's mind (to do something)
der **Vorsatz, ⸗e** plan; resolution

vor-schlagen* to propose, suggest; **der Vorschlag, ⸗e** suggestion
vorsichtig *adj.* careful, cautious
die **Vorstellung, -en** performance (theater)
der **Vortrag, ⸗e** lecture; recitation
vorübergehend *adj.* passing, transitory

W

wachsen, wuchs, ist gewachsen, er wächst to grow
der **Wagen, -** wagon; auto
wählen to choose; vote, elect; **die Wahl, -en** election
wahr *adj.* true, real; **nicht wahr?** isn't it so?
während *prep. gen.* during; *conj.* while
wahrhaft *adv.* truly, really
die **Wahrheit, -en** truth
wahrscheinlich *adv.* probably
der **Wald, ⸗er** forest, woods
die **Wand, ⸗e** wall
wandern, ist gewandert to wander, travel
die **Wandtafel, -n** blackboard
wann *interr. and conj.* when
die **Ware, -n** goods, merchandise
warm *adj.* warm
warnen to warn, caution
warten to wait; **warten auf** to wait for *with acc.*
warum *interr.* why
was *interr.* what; *rel. pron.* whatever, that
waschen, wusch, gewaschen, er wäscht to wash
das **Wasser, -** water; river
der **Wasserstoff** hydrogen
Weber, C. J. German writer and historian, 1767–1832
weder . . . noch *conj.* neither . . . nor
der **Weg, -e** road, way
wegen *prep. gen.* because of, on account of
wehen to blow
weich *adj.* soft, mild
sich **weigern** to decline, refuse
weil *conj.* because, since

der **Wein, -e** wine
weinen to weep, cry
weise *adj.* wise, prudent; **die Weisheit** wisdom, prudence; philosophy
die **Weise, -n** manner, way; **in dieser Weise** in this way
weiß *adj.* white
weit *adj.* distant, far away; broad, spacious; **es weit bringen** to get on (in the world)
weiter *adv.* farther, further; **und so weiter** and so on
welcher, welche, welches *interr. pron. and rel. pron.* which, what; who, which
die **Welt, -en** world; universe; **auf der Welt** on earth; **alle Welt** everybody
wem *dat. of interr. and rel. pron.* **wer** to whom
wen *acc. of interr. and rel. pron.* **wer** whom
wenden, wandte, gewandt, er wendet to turn
wenig *adj.* little; *pl.* a few
wenn *conj.* when, whenever, if; **als wenn** as if; **wenn auch** even if
wer *interr. and rel. pron.* who, whoever, he who
werden, wurde, geworden, er wird to become, grow, get; *as fut. aux.* shall, will; *as passive aux.* to be
werfen, warf, geworfen, er wirft to throw
das **Werk, -e** work; books
der **Wert, -e** value
das **Wetter, -** weather
wichtig *adj.* important
wider = **gegen** *prep. acc.* against, contrary to
wie *interr. adv. and conj.* how, as, such as; **wieviel?** how much? **wie viele?** how many?
wieder *adv.* again
wieder-sehen* to see (meet) again; **auf Wiedersehen!** till we meet again! goodbye!
der **Wille, -ns, -n** will; **aus freiem Willen** voluntarily; **mit Willen** on purpose

willkommen *adj.* welcome
der **Wind, -e** wind
windig *adj.* windy, drafty
der **Winter, -** winter; **den Winter über** through the winter
wirklich *adv.* really, truly
der **Wirt, -e** host; innkeeper
das **Wirtshaus, ⸗er** inn
wissen, wußte, gewußt, er weiß to know; **das Wissen** knowledge
die **Wissenschaft, -en** science, learning
die **Witwe, -n** widow
der **Witz, -e** joke; intelligence, wit, power of the mind
wo *interr. adv. and conj.* where
wobei *adv.* through which, by so doing
die **Woche, -n** week; **eine Woche lang** for a week; **wochenlang** for weeks
wodurch *adv.* by which
wofür *adv.* for what, what for
woher *adv.* from where
wohin *adv.* where to
wohl *adj. and adv.* well; perhaps, possibly
der **Wohllaut** harmony, melody
das **Wohlwollen** kindness
die **Wohnung, -en** = **das Wohnhaus, ⸗er** house, residence
der **Wohnzweck: nicht zu Wohnzwecken bestimmt** not intended as living quarters
die **Wolke, -n** cloud
wollen, wollte, gewollt, er will *mod. aux.* will, wish, want to
woran = **an was** *adv.* whereon; against what
worauf *adv.* whereupon, upon which
woraus *adv.* out of which
das **Wort, ⸗er** *or* **-e** word; **Wort halten** to keep a promise
das **Wörterbuch, ⸗er** dictionary
wovon *adv.* from what
wozu *adv.* what for
wünschen to wish; der **Wunsch, ⸗e** wish

Z

die **Zahl, -en** number
zahlen to pay
zählen to count

zeigen to show
die **Zeile, -n** line
die **Zeit, -en** time; period, age; **eine Zeitlang** for a time; **vor langer Zeit** long time ago; **zur Zeit** at present; **aus alten Zeiten** from olden times; **zu allen Zeiten** always, at any time
die **Zeitung, -en** newspaper
zensieren to grade
zerbrechen* to break to pieces
zerreißen* to tear to pieces
zerschneiden* to cut up
zerspringen* to burst, crash to pieces
zerstören to destroy
der **Zeuge, -n** witness
ziehen, zog, hat gezogen, es zieht to draw, pull; **zog, ist gezogen, er zieht** to move
das **Ziel, -e** aim, objective; destination
ziemlich *adv.* rather, quite
die **Zigarette, -n** cigarette

das **Zimmer, -** room
zu *prep. dat.* to, on, at, for; *adv.* too
zuerst *adv.* at first
zufällig *adj. and adv.* accidentally
zufrieden *adj.* content, satisfied
der **Zug, ⸗e** train
zu-hören to listen to
die **Zukunft** future
zuletzt *adv.* finally, last, at last
zu-messen to allot, mete out
zurück *adv. and sep. pref.* back
zurück-kehren, ist zurückgekehrt to return
zurück-schicken to send back, return
zuweilen *adv.* at times
zwar *adv.* I admit, to be sure
zweifeln to doubt; der **Zweifel** doubt
zweimal *adv.* twice
zweitens *adv.* secondly, in the second place
zwischen *prep. dat. or acc.* between

English-German Vocabulary

A

a, an ein, eine, ein; **not a** kein, keine, kein

able: to be able können *mod. aux.*

about ungefähr *adv.;* von *prep. dat.;* über *prep. acc.;* **to talk about** sprechen von, sprechen über

account: on account of wegen *prep. gen.*

accustom sich gewöhnen

across über *prep. acc.*

act tun; **he acts as if** er tut, als ob

address die Adresse, -en

afraid: to be afraid sich fürchten vor *with dat.*

after nach *prep. dat.;* **after dinner** nach dem Essen; **after school** nach der Schule

afternoon der Nachmittag, -e; **one afternoon** eines Nachmittags; **in the afternoon** nachmittags

again wieder *adv.*

against gegen *prep. acc.*

all alle, alles; ganz; **not at all** gar nicht; **all day** den ganzen Tag

allowed: to be allowed dürfen *mod. aux.;* **I am not allowed** ich darf nicht

along mit *adv.;* **to go along** mit-gehen; **to bring along** mit-bringen

although obgleich *conj.*

always immer *adv.*

answer antworten *with dat. o. p.;* beantworten *with direct obj. of things*

are: du bist, wir sind, ihr seid, sie sind, Sie sind

army das Heer, -e; die Armee, Armeen

arrive ankommen, ist angekommen

artist der Künstler, -

as (*conj.*) da; (*in comparison*) wie; **as if** als ob; **as soon as** sobald als; **as long as** solange

ask fragen, bitten; **to ask a question** eine Frage stellen

assemble sich versammeln

at an, auf, in, bei, zu *prep. dat.;* **at home** zu Hause; **at night** nachts; **at the university** auf der Universität

away fort, weg *adv.*

B

bad schlecht *adj.*

be sein, war, ist gewesen, es ist

beautiful schön

because weil *conj.;* **because of** wegen *prep. gen.*

become werden, wurde, ist geworden, es wird

bed das Bett, -en

before ehe *conj.*

believe glauben *with dat. o. p. and acc. of things;* **I believe him** ich glaube ihm; **I believe it** ich glaube es

bell die Glocke, -n

belong to gehören *with dat.;* **it belongs to me** es gehört mir

below unter *prep. dat. or acc.*

beside neben *prep. dat. or acc.*

best am besten *superlative of* gut; **the best** das Beste

birthday der Geburtstag, -e

black schwarz *adj.*

blackboard die Wandtafel, -n; **at the blackboard** an der Wandtafel; **to the blackboard** an die Wandtafel

Bonn: capital city of West Germany

book das Buch, ⸗er

boy der Junge, -n, -n

bracelet das Armband, ⸗er

break brechen, zerbrechen

bring bringen, brachte, gebracht, er bringt; **bring along** mit-bringen

brother der Bruder, ⸗

building das Gebäude, -

business das Geschäft, -e

busy beschäftigt

but aber, sondern *conj.*

buy kaufen

C

call rufen, rief, hat gerufen, er ruft; nennen, nannte, genannt, er nennt; **to be called** heißen, hieß, geheißen, er heißt

can kömmen *mod. aux.;* **cannot** kann nicht

care for mögen *mod. aux.;* **I don't care to** ich will nicht
careful sorgfältig, vorsichtig
carry tragen; **to carry out** aus-führen
catch fangen; **to catch cold** sich erkälten
certainly gewiß, sicher *adv.*
chair der Stuhl, ⸗e
child das Kind, -er
church die Kirche -n; **in church** in der Kirche
city die Stadt, ⸗e; **of our city** unserer Stadt
city hall das Rathaus, ⸗er
class die Klasse, -n
clean sauber, rein *adj.*
clear klar; evident
clock die Uhr, -en; **at six o'clock** um sechs Uhr
close zu-machen, schließen; **I am closing** ich mache zu
closet der Kleiderschrank, ⸗e
cold kalt, kälter, am kältesten; **to catch cold** sich erkälten
color die Farbe, -n
colorful bunt *adj.*
come kommen, ist gekommen, er kommt; **is not coming** kommt nicht; **to come along** mit-kommen; **to come home** nach Hause kommen
concert das Konzert, -e
cool kühl *adj.*
could konnte *mod. aux.;* **would be able to** könnte
country das Land, ⸗er; **in the country** auf dem Lande

D

dance der Tanz, ⸗e
dark dunkel *adj.*
daughter die Tochter, ⸗
day der Tag, -e; **some day** eines Tages; **one day** eines Tages; **three days ago** vor drei Tagen
daylight: at daylight am Tage
dear lieb; **dear mother** liebe Mutter
deceive betrügen
deep tief *adj.*
degree der Grad, -e
deny leugnen

did: did you? hast du? Haben Sie? **did you have?** haben Sie gehabt? **did he come?** ist er gekommen?
die sterben
diligent fleißig; **diligence** der Fleiß
do tun, tat, getan; **how do you do?** wie geht es Ihnen? **I didn't do it** ich habe es nicht getan; **do you know?** weißt du? kennst du? kennen Sie?
dog der Hund, -e
door die Tür, -en
doubt zweifeln
dress an-ziehen; das Kleid, -er
drive fahren
during während *prep. gen.*

E

early früh
east der Osten; Orient
either auch nicht *adv.*
end das Ende, -n; **at one end** an einem Ende
enter ein-treten, herein-kommen; **to enter the room** ins Zimmer treten
even if selbst *adv.*
evening der Abend, -e; **one evening** eines Abends; **evenings** abends; **in the evening** am Abend
every jeder, jede, jedes
everything alles
examination die Prüfung, -en
expensive teuer

F

face das Gesicht, -er
faithful treu
family die Familie, -n
famous berühmt *adj.*
farmer der Bauer, -n
father der Vater, ⸗
few wenig, wenige; **a few** einige, wenige
field das Feld, -er
find finden
finger der Finger, -
finish beenden, fertig-machen; **finished** fertig
first erst; **at first** zuerst; **the first time** das erste Mal
flower die Blume, -n

follow folgen, ist gefolgt *with dat. of pers.*
foot der Fuß, -es, ⸗e **at the foot of** am Fuße eines
football der Fußball, ⸗e
for für *prep. acc.; **for money** für Geld; **for the first time** zum ersten Mal
foreign fremd; **the foreigner** der Fremde
forget vergessen
found fand, hat gefunden, *past of* finden
freedom die Freiheit, -en
freeze frieren; **the freezing point** der Gefrierpunkt, -e
friend der Freund, -e
front: in front of vor

G

garden der Garten, ⸗
gather sammeln; sich versammeln
gentleman der Herr, -n, -en
German *(language)* Deutsch; *adj.* deutsch; **in German** auf deutsch
Germany (das) Deutschland
get *(to receive)* erhalten, bekommen; *(to become)* werden; **to get angry** sich ärgern; **to get rich** reich werden; **to get up** auf-stehen
gift das Geschenk, -e
girl das Mädchen, -; **girl friend** die Freundin, -nen
give geben; *(to present)* schenken
go gehen, ist gegangen; **I am going** ich gehe; **to go to school** zur Schule gehen; **to go home** nach Hause gehen; **to go along** mit-gehen
good gut, besser, am besten *adj.*
grandparents die Großeltern *pl.*
great groß, größer, am größten *adj.*
grow wachsen, ist gewachsen
guest der Gast, ⸗e

H

hair das Haar, -e
half halb; die Hälfte; **at half past nine** um halb zehn
hand die Hand, ⸗e; **to hand in** ein-reichen
hang hängen
happy glücklich *adj.*

hard schwer; hart, härter, am härtesten; **to work hard** schwer arbeiten; **to study hard** fleißig studieren
harm schaden *with dat.*
has to er muß *(mod. aux.* müssen)
have haben, hatte, gehabt, er hat; **I have to** ich muß; **I have to stay home** ich muß zu Hause bleiben; **I had to do it** ich mußte es tun
he er *pers. pron.;* **he who** wer *indef. pron.*
head der Kopf, ⸗e; **at the head of** an der Spitze von
health die Gesundheit, -en
hear hören; **I heard him sing** ich habe ihn singen hören
help helfen, half, geholfen, er hilft *with dat.;* die Hilfe, -n
her ihr *(dat)*, sie *(acc.) of pers. pron.* sie
her ihr, ihre, ihr *poss. pron.*
here hier *adv.*
high hoch, höher, an höchsten *adj.*
hill der Hügel, -
him ihm *(dat.)*, ihn *(acc.) of pers. pron.* er
his sein, seine, sein *poss. pron.*
home das Haus, ⸗er; **at home** zu Hause; **to go home** nach Hause gehen
homework die Schularbeit, -en
horse das Pferd, -e
hot heiß *adj.*
hour die Stunde, -n; **at what hour?** um welche Stunde? um welche Zeit?
house das Haus, ⸗er; **at our house** in unserm Haus
how wie *inter.;* **how much?** wieviel; **how many** wie viele; **how do you do?** wie geht es Ihnen?
hurry sich beeilen

I

I ich *pers. pron.;* **I am** ich bin
immediately gleich, sofort
in in *prep. dat. or acc.*
influential einflußreich *adj.*
ink die Tinte, -n
innocent unschuldig *adj.*
inside of innerhalb *prep. gen.*
in spite of trotz *prep. gen.*
instead of statt, anstatt *prep. gen.*
interested: to be interested in sich interessieren für *with acc.*

interesting interessant *adj.*
into in *prep. acc.*
it (*masc.*) er; (*fem.*) sie; (*neut.*) es; **who
is it?** wer ist's? **it is I** ich bin's

J

judge der Richter, -
just eben, gerade *adv.*

K

keep behalten
kind (dear, beloved) freundlich; **please,
be so kind,** bitte seien Sie so freundlich
king der König, -e
knock klopfen
know (*a fact*) wissen, wußte, gewußt, er
weiß; (*to be acquainted with*) kennen,
kannte, gekannt, er kennt; **do you
know the man?** kennen Sie den Mann?
do you know where he lives? wissen
Sie, wo er wohnt?

L

lady die Dame, -n; die Frau, -en
lake der See, Se-es, Se-en
lame lahm *adj.*
large groß, größer, am größten *adj.*
last letzt-; **last summer** im letzten
Sommer
late spät
law das Gesetz, -e
lazy faul, träge *adj.*
leave lassen; (*to depart*) ab-fahren, ab-
reisen; **let it go** laß es gehen
lecture die Vorlesung, -en
lesson die Aufgabe, -n
let lassen; **let's go!** gehen wir!
letter der Brief, -e
lie liegen, ruhen
lie (*to tell a lie*) lügen, log, gelogen, er
lügt; **he is lying** er lügt
like gern haben; **like to** mögen; **I like to
play** ich spiele gern; **I don't like it** es
gefällt mir nicht
little (*size*) klein; (*quantity*) wenig
live leben; (*dwell*) wohnen
load die Last, -en

long (*adj.*) lang; (*adv.*) lange; **how long?**
wie lange?
longing sich sehnen
look sehen; (*appear*) aus-sehen; **to look
for** suchen; **to look at** an-sehen
lose verlieren
loud laut *adj.*
love lieben, lieb-haben

M

man der Mann, =er; (*human being*) der
Mensch, -en, -en
many viele; **many a** mancher
map die Landkarte, -n
market der Markt, =e; **to the market** auf
den Markt
master der Herr, -n, -en
may dürfen *mod. aux.;* mögen *mod. aux.;*
may I go? darf ich gehen?
me (*dat.*) mir; (*acc.*) mich *of pers. pron.*
ich
meet begegnen, ist begegnet *with dat.;*
treffen *with acc.;* **I met her** ich
begegnete ihr; ich traf sie
miss vermissen; (*to omit*) aus-lassen
mistake der Fehler, -; der Irrtum, =er
money das Geld, -er
monotonous eintönig, langweilig
month der Monat, -e
morning der Morgen -; **this morning**
heute morgen; **in the morning**
morgens; **early morning** früh morgens
most meist, höchst
mother die Mutter, =
mountain der Berg, -e
much (*quantity*) viel; (*degree*) sehr; **how
much?** wieviel? **very much** sehr viel
music die Musik
must müssen *mod. aux.*
my mein, meine, mein *poss. adj.*

N

name der Name, -n; **what is your name?**
Wie heißen Sie?
narrow eng *adj.*
need brauchen
neighbor der Nachbar, -s, -n
neither . . . nor weder . . . noch *conj.*
never nie, niemals *adv.*

new neu *adj.*
newspaper die Zeitung, -en
next nächst; **next to** neben *prep. dat. or acc.*
night die Nacht, ⸗e; **at night** in der Nacht; **last night** gestern abend; **nights** nachts
no nein; kein, keine, kein
nobody niemand
noon der Mittag, -e; **at noon** mittags
not nicht; **not a** kein; **not at all** gar nicht; **not yet** noch nicht
now jetzt *adv.*
number die Nummer, -n

O

obey gehorchen *with dat.*
ocean der Ozean, -e; das Meer, -e
o'clock: **at six o'clock** um sechs Uhr
of von *prep. dat.*
often oft *adv.*
old alt, älter, am ältesten *adj.*
on auf, an *prep. dat. or acc.*
once einmal; **once more** noch einmal; **once upon a time** einmal
only nur *adv.*
or oder *conj.*
other ander-; der (die, das) andere, die anderen *pron.*
our unser, unsere, unser *poss. adj.*
out hinaus, heraus *with verbs of motion;* **out of the house** aus dem Haus heraus; **school is out** die Schule ist aus
outside of außerhalb *prep. gen.*
over über *prep. dat. or acc.*
overcoat der Mantel, ⸗

P

package das Paket, -e
page die Seite, -n
paint malen, (*a house*) an-streichen
painting das Bild, -er; das Gemälde, -
paper das Papier, -e; **newspaper** die Zeitung, -en
parents die Eltern *pl.*
penny der Pfennig, -e
people die Leute *pl.;* die Menschen *pl.*
permission die Erlaubnis, -se
permit erlauben

personal persönlich *adv.*
physician der Arzt, ⸗e
place der Platz, ⸗e; der Ort, -e; die Stelle, -n; **in your place** an deiner Stelle
play spielen; das Spiel, -e
please! bitte!
poem das Gedicht, -e
poor arm, ärmer, am ärmsten; **poor work** schlechte Arbeit
post office das Postamt, ⸗er; **to the post-office** zur Post
powerful mächtig *adj.*
prepare vor-bereiten
present die Gegenwart; **at present** gegenwärtig, augenblicklich *adv.*
print drucken
prove beweisen
put legen, stellen, setzen, stecken

Q

quaint wunderlich, seltsam *adj.*
question fragen, die Frage, -n
questioning fragend *pres. part.*
quiet still
quite ganz *adv.;* **quite often** sehr oft

R

rain regnen; der Regen, -
rapidly schnell
read lesen
readily gern, bereitwillig *adv.*
ready fertig, bereit
receive erhalten; (*to welcome*) empfangen, auf-nehmen
recognize erkennen, er erkennt
remarkable außerordentlich, beachtenswert *adj.*
remember sich erinnern *with gen.*
report berichten; der Bericht, -e
representative der Vertreter, -
request die Bitte, -n
respect der Respekt; respektieren
rest ruhen; die Ruhe, -n
return zurück-kommen, ist zurückgekommen; **return home** nach Hause kommen
Rhein: name of a river
rich reich *adj.*

ring der Ring, -e; **to ring the bells** die Glocken läuten

river der Fluß, Flusses, Flüsse

road der Weg, -e

room das Zimmer, -

row rudern, ist gerudert

S

same: the same derselbe, dieselbe, dasselbe

say sagen; **said to be** soll sein

school die Schule, -n; **in school** in der Schule; **to school** zur Schule

see sehen; sprechen *with acc.*

sell verkaufen

serve dienen *with dat.*

severe hart, streng, schwer *adj.*

shall werden *aux. of fut. tenses;* sollen, müssen *mod. aux.;* **I shall write** ich werde schreiben

she sie *pers. pron.*

ship das Schiff, -e

short kurz, kürzer, am kürzesten *adj.*

should sollen *mod. aux.;* **he should go** er soll gehen

show zeigen

sick krank, kränker, am kränkesten *adj.*

sickness die Krankheit, -en

side die Seite, -n; **on this side of** diesseits *prep. gen.*

since seit *prep. dat.;* da, weil *conj.*

single einzig; einzeln

sister die Schwester, -n

sit sitzen; **to sit down** sich setzen

sleep schlafen

slender schlank; groß

slow langsam

smart klug, klüger, am klügsten *adj.*

smoke rauchen; der Rauch

snow schneien; der Schnee

soft leise *adv.;* weich *adj.*

some etwas, einige; **some day** eines Tages

somebody jemand

sometime einmal, manchmal

son der Sohn, ≃e

sorry: **I am sorry** es tut mir leid

south der Süden

speak sprechen, reden

stand stehen

stay bleiben, ist geblieben; sich aufhalten; **to stay at home** zu Hause bleiben

steep steil *adj.*

still noch *adv.*

stop auf-hören

storm der Sturm, ≃e, das Gewitter, -

story die Geschichte, -n

stove der Ofen, ≃; **by the stove** am Ofen

stranger der Fremde, -n

street die Straße, -n; **in the street** auf der Straße

strong stark, stärker, am stärksten

student der Student, -en; die Studentin, -nen

study studieren, lernen; die Studie, Studien; **the study** das Studium, Studien; das Studierzimmer

stupid dumm, dümmer, am dümmsten

succeed gelingen, ist gelungen; **I do not succeed** es gelingt mir nicht

success der Erfolg, -e

such solcher, solche, solches, solch

summer der Sommer, -; **in summer** im Sommer

sun die Sonne, -n; **the sun rises** die Sonne geht auf; **the sun sets** die Sonne geht unter

Sunday der Sonntag, -e; **on Sunday** sonntags, am Sonntag

surprise: **to be surprised at** sich wundern über *with acc.;* **surprised** überrascht, erstaunt

suspect vermuten

swim schwimmen, ist geschwommen

T

table der Tisch, -e

take nehmen, bringen, machen; **to take away** weg-nehmen; **I'll take you home** ich bringe dich nach Hause; **to take a walk** einen Spaziergang machen

talk sprechen; **to talk about** sprechen über *with acc.;* sprechen von *with dat.*

tall hoch, höher, am höchsten; groß, größer, am größten

teacher der Lehrer, -; die Lehrerin, -nen

tell erzählen, sagen; **tell me** sage mir

test die Prüfung, -en

thank danken

that das; **that one** der, jener *dem. pron.;*
der, welcher *rel. pron.;* daß *conj.*
theater das Theater, -; **to go to the theater** ins Theater gehen; **at the theater**
im Theater
their ihr, ihre, ihr *poss. pron.*
them *(dat.)* ihnen; *(acc.)* sie; *of pers.
pron.* sie
there da, dort; **there is, there are** es gibt,
es sind; **there was** es war
these diese *pl.*
they sie *pers. pron.*
think denken; **to think of** denken an
with acc. **do you think** denkst du,
denken Sie
this dieser, diese, dieses, dies; **this morning** heute morgen
those jene *pl.*
thrifty sparsam *adj.*
till = **until** bis *prep. and conj.*
time die Zeit, -en; **first time** das erste
Mal; **what time is it?** wie spät ist es?
at what time? um welche Zeit?
tired müde *adj.*
to zu, nach *prep. dat.;* auf, in, an *prep.
acc.;* **to go to school** zur Schule gehen;
to the theater ins Theater
today heute *adv.*
together zusammen *adv.*
tomorrow morgen *adv.* **tomorrow morning** morgen früh
tonight heute abend
too auch, ebenfalls, zu *adv.* **too much** zu
viel
town die Stadt, ⸗e; **in town** in der Stadt
travel reisen, ist gereist
tree der Baum, ⸗e
true wahr *adj.* *(faithful)* treu
truth die Wahrheit, -en
try versuchen

U

under unter *prep. dat. or acc.*
understand verstehen
unhappy unglücklich
university die Universität, -en; **at the
university** auf der Universität
unprepared unvorbereitet *adj.*
until bis *prep. and conj.*

us uns *dat. or acc. of pers. pron.* wir
usually gewöhnlich *adv.*

V

very sehr *adv.;* **very much** sehr, sehr viel;
very well sehr gut
visit besuchen; der Besuch, -e
voice die Stimme, -n

W

walk gehen, ist gegangen
walk der Spaziergang, ⸗e; **to take a walk**
einen Spaziergang machen
want wollen *mod. aux.;* **what do you
want?** was wollen Sie?
war der Krieg, -e
warm warm, wärmer, am wärmsten *adj.*
watch die Uhr, -en
we wir *pers. pron.*
wear tragen, trug, getragen, er trägt
weather das Wetter
week die Woche, -n; **a week ago** vor
einer Woche
well gut, besser, am besten; **I am well** ich
bin gesund, es geht mir gut
what was *interr. and rel. pron.;* **what kind
of?** was für ein?
when wann *interr. adv. and conj.;* *(for
definite past action)* als; *(as conj.)* wenn
whenever wenn *conj.*
where wo *interr. pron.;* **where have you
been?** wo bist du gewesen?
whether ob *conj.*
which der, die, das *rel. pron.;* welcher,
welche, welches *rel. and interr. pron.
and interr. adj.*
while: **wait a while** warten Sie eine Weile,
warten Sie einen Augenblick
while während *conj.*
white weiß *adj.*
who wer *inter. and rel. pron.;* der, die,
das; welcher, welche, welches *rel.
pron.*
whole ganz; **the whole evening** den
ganzen Abend
whom *(interr.)* wem *with dat. or acc.;*
(rel. pron.) dem, der, dem; **to whom?**
wem? **for whom?** für wen? **with whom?**
mit wem?

whose (*rel. pron.*) dessen, deren, dessen; *pl.* deren; (*inter.*) wessen?

why warum *interr.*

wide breit, weit *adj.*

will werden *aux. for fut. tenses;* wollen *mod. aux. to express wish or willingness;* **it will be** es wird sein

window das Fenster, -; **at (by) the window** am Fenster

winter der Winter, -

wish wünschen; der Wunsch, ⸚e; wollen *mod. aux.*

with mit, bei *prep. dat.*

within innerhalb *prep. gen.*

without ohne *prep. acc.*

woman die Frau, -en

work arbeiten; **to work hard** schwer arbeiten; **out of work** ohne Arbeit, arbeitslos

world die Welt, -en

would würde; **he would have** er würde haben

write schreiben; **writer** der Schriftsteller, -

Y

year das Jahr, -e; **for three years** seit drei Jahren

yesterday gestern; **day before yesterday** vorgestern

you (*nom.*) du, ihr, Sir; (*dat.*) dir, euch, Ihnen; (*acc.*) dich, euch, Sie

young jung, jünger, am jüngsten

your dein, deine, dein; euer, eure, euer; Ihr, Ihre, Ihr

Index

References are to pages